The **Essential** Buyer's Guide

SUBARU
IMPREZA
All turbo models 1992 to 2007

Your marque expert:
David Hobbs

GW00585513

VELOCE PUBLISHING
THE PUBLISHER OF FINE AUTOMOTIVE BOOKS

Also from Veloce Publishing

Speedpro Series
4-cylinder Engine – How To Blueprint & Build A Short Block For High Performance (Hammill)
Alfa Romeo DOHC High-performance Manual (Kartalamakis)
Alfa Romeo V6 Engine High-performance Manual (Kartalamakis)
BMC 998cc A-series Engine – How To Power Tune (Hammill)
1275cc A-series High-performance Manual (Hammill)
Camshafts – How To Choose & Time Them For Maximum Power (Hammill)
Competition Car Datalogging Manual, The (Templeman)
Cylinder Heads – How To Build, Modify & Power Tune Updated & Revised Edition (Burgess & Gollan)
Distributor-type Ignition Systems – How To Build & Power Tune (Hammill)
Fast Road Car – How To Plan And Build Revised & Updated Colour New Edition (Stapleton)
Ford SOHC 'Pinto' & Sierra Cosworth DOHC Engines – How To Power Tune Updated & Enlarged Edition (Hammill)
Ford V8 – How To Power Tune Small Block Engines (Hammill)
Harley-Davidson Evolution Engines – How To Build & Power Tune (Hammill)
Holley Carburetors – How To Build & Power Tune Revised & Updated Edition (Hammill)
Jaguar XK Engines – How To Power Tune Revised & Updated Colour Edition (Hammill)
MG Midget & Austin-Healey Sprite – How To Power Tune Updated & Revised Edition (Stapleton)
MGB 4-cylinder Engine – How To Power Tune (Burgess)
MGB V8 Power – How To Give Your, Third Colour Edition (Williams)
MGB, MGC & MGB V8 – How To Improve (Williams)
Mini Engines – How To Power Tune On A Small Budget Colour Edition (Hammill)
Motorcycle-engined Racing Car – How To Build (Pashley)
Motorsport – Getting Started in (Collins)
Nitrous Oxide High-performance Manual, The (Langfield)
Rover V8 Engines – How To Power Tune (Hammill)
Sportscar/kitcar Suspension & Brakes – How To Build & Modify Enlarged & Updated 2nd Edition (Hammill)
SU Carburettor High-performance Manual (Hammill)
Supercar, How To Build (Thompson)
Suzuki 4x4 – How To Modify For Serious Off-road Action (Richardson)
Tiger Avon Sportscar – How To Build Your Own Updated & Revised 2nd Edition (Dudley)
TR2, 3 & TR4 – How To Improve (Williams)
TR5, 250 & TR6 – How To Improve (Williams)
TR7 & TR8 – How To Improve (Williams)
V8 Engine – How To Build A Short Block For High Performance (Hammill)
Volkswagen Beetle Suspension, Brakes & Chassis – How To Modify For High Performance (Hale)
Volkswagen Bus Suspension, Brakes & Chassis – How To Modify For High Performance (Hale)
Weber DCOE, & Dellorto DHLA Carburetors – How To Build & Power Tune 3rd Edition (Hammill)

Those Were The Days ... Series
Alpine Trials & Rallies 1910-1973 (Pfundner)
Austerity Motoring (Bobbitt)
Brighton National Speed Trials (Gardiner)
British Police Cars (Walker)
British Woodies (Peck)
Dune Buggy Phenomenon (Hale)
Dune Buggy Phenomenon Volume 2 (Hale)
Hot Rod & Stock Car Racing in Britain In The 1980s (Neil)
MG's Abingdon Factory (Moylan)
Motor Racing At Brands Hatch In The Seventies (Parker)
Motor Racing At Crystal Palace (Collins)
Motor Racing At Goodwood In The Sixties (Gardiner)
Motor Racing At Nassau In The 1950s & 1960s (O'Neil)
Motor Racing At Oulton Park In The 1960s (Mcfadyen)
Motor Racing At Oulton Park In The 1970s (Mcfadyen)
Three Wheelers (Bobbitt)

Enthusiast's Restoration Manual Series
Citroën 2CV, How To Restore (Porter)
Classic Car Bodywork, How To Restore (Thaddeus)
Classic Car Electrics (Thaddeus)
Classic Cars, How To Paint (Thaddeus)
Reliant Regal, How To Restore (Payne)
Triumph TR2/3/3A, How To Restore (Williams)
Triumph TR4/4A, How To Restore (Williams)
Triumph TR5/250 & 6, How To Restore (Williams)
Triumph TR7/8, How To Restore (Williams)
Volkswagen Beetle, How To Restore (Tyler)
VW Bay Window Bus (Paxton)
Yamaha FS1-E, How To Restore (Watts)

Essential Buyer's Guide Series
Alfa GT (Booker)
Alfa Romeo Spider Giulia (Booker & Talbott)
BMW GS (Henshaw)
BSA Bantam (Henshaw)
BSA Twins (Henshaw)
Citroën 2CV (Paxton)
Citroën ID & DS (Heilig)
Fiat 500 & 600 (Bobbitt)
Jaguar E-type 3.8 & 4.2-litre (Crespin)
Jaguar E-type V12 5.3-litre (Crespin)
Jaguar/Daimler XJ6, XJ12 & Sovereign (Crespin)
Jaguar XJ-S (Crespin)
MGB & MGB GT (Williams)
Mercedes-Benz 280SL-560DSL Roadsters (Bass)
Mercedes-Benz 'Pagoda' 230SL, 250SL & 280SL Roadsters & Coupés (Bass)
Morris Minor & 1000 (Newell)
Porsche 928 (Hemmings)
Rolls-Royce Silver Shadow & Bentley T-Series (Bobbitt)
Subaru Impreza (Hobbs)
Triumph Bonneville (Henshaw)
Triumph TR6 (Williams)
VW Beetle (Cservenka & Copping)
VW Bus (Cservenka & Copping)

Auto-Graphics Series
Fiat-based Abarths (Sparrow)
Jaguar MKI & II Saloons (Sparrow)
Lambretta Li Series Scooters (Sparrow)

Rally Giants Series
Audi Quattro (Robson)
Austin Healey 100-6 & 3000 (Robson)
Fiat 131 Abarth (Robson)
Ford Escort MkI (Robson)
Ford Escort RS Cosworth & World Rally Car (Robson)
Ford Escort RS1800 (Robson)
Lancia Stratos (Robson)
Peugeot 205 T16 (Robson)
Subaru Impreza (Robson)

General
1½-litre GP Racing 1961-1965 (Whitelock)
AC Two-litre Saloons & Buckland Sportscars (Archibald)
Alfa Romeo Giulia Coupé GT & GTA (Tipler)
Alfa Romeo Montreal – The Essential Companion (Taylor)
Alfa Tipo 33 (McDonough & Collins)
Alpine & Renault – The Development Of The Revolutionary Turbo F1 Car 1968 to 1979 (Smith)
Anatomy Of The Works Minis (Moylan)
Armstrong-Siddeley (Smith)
Autodrome (Collins & Ireland)
Automotive A-Z, Lane's Dictionary Of Automotive Terms (Lane)
Automotive Mascots (Kay & Springate)
Bahamas Speed Weeks, The (O'Neil)
Bentley Continental, Corniche And Azure (Bennett)
Bentley MkVI, Rolls-Royce Silver Wraith, Dawn & Cloud/ Bentley R & S-Series (Nutland)
BMC Competitions Department Secrets (Turner, Chambers Browning)
BMW 5-Series (Cranswick)
BMW Z-Cars (Taylor)
Britains Farm Model Balers & Combines 1967 to 2007 (Pullen)
British 250cc Racing Motorcycles (Pereira)
British Cars, The Complete Catalogue Of, 1895-1975 (Culshaw & Horrobin)
BRM – A Mechanic's Tale (Salmon)
BRM V16 (Ludvigsen)
BSA Bantam Bible, The (Henshaw)
Bugatti Type 40 (Price)
Bugatti 46/50 Updated Edition (Price & Arbey)
Bugatti T44 & T49 (Price & Arbey)
Bugatti 57 2nd Edition (Price)
Caravans, The Illustrated History 1919-1959 (Jenkinson)
Caravans, The Illustrated History From 1960 (Jenkinson)
Carrera Panamericana, La (Tipler)
Chrysler 300 – America's Most Powerful Car 2nd Edition (Ackerson)
Chrysler PT Cruiser (Ackerson)
Citroën DS (Bobbitt)
Cliff Allison – From The Fells To Ferrari (Gauld)
Cobra – The Real Thing! (Legate)
Cortina – Ford's Bestseller (Robson)
Coventry Climax Racing Engines (Hammill)
Daimler SP250 New Edition (Long)
Datsun Fairlady Roadster To 280ZX – The Z-Car Story (Long)
Dino – The V6 Ferrari (Long)
Dodge Charger – Enduring Thunder (Ackerson)
Dodge Dynamite! (Grist)
Donington (Boddy)
Draw & Paint Cars – How To (Gardiner)
Drive On The Wild Side, A – 20 Extreme Driving Adventures From Around The World (Weaver)
Ducati 750 Bible, The (Falloon)
Ducati 860, 900 And Mille Bible, The (Falloon)
Dune Buggy, Building A – The Essential Manual (Shakespeare)
Dune Buggy Files (Hale)
Dune Buggy Handbook (Hale)
Edward Turner: The Man Behind The Motorcycles (Clew)
Fiat & Abarth 124 Spider & Coupé (Tipler)
Fiat & Abarth 500 & 600 2nd Edition (Bobbitt)
Fiats, Great Small (Ward)
Fine Art Of The Motorcycle Engine, The (Peirce)
Ford F100/F150 Pick-up 1948-1996 (Ackerson)
Ford F150 Pick-up 1997-2005 (Ackerson)
Ford GT – Then, And Now (Streather)
Ford GT40 (Legate)
Ford In Miniature (Olson)
Ford Model Y (Roberts)
Ford Thunderbird From 1954, The Book Of The (Long)
Forza Minardi! (Vigar)
Funky Mopeds (Skelton)
Gentleman Jack (Gauld)
GM In Miniature (Olson)
GT – The World's Best GT Cars 1953-73 (Dawson)
Hillclimbing & Sprinting – The Essential Manual (Short & Wilkinson)
Honda NSX (Long)
Jaguar, The Rise Of (Price)
Jaguar XJ-S (Long)
Jeep CJ (Ackerson)
Jeep Wrangler (Ackerson)
Karmann-Ghia Coupé & Convertible (Bobbitt)
Lamborghini Miura Bible, The (Sackey)
Lambretta Bible, The (Davies)
Lancia 037 (Collins)
Lancia Delta HF Integrale (Blaettel & Wagner)
Land Rover, The Half-ton Military (Cook)
Laverda Twins & Triples Bible 1968-1986 (Falloon)
Lea-Francis Story, The (Price)
Lexus Story, The (Long)
little book of smart, the (Jackson)
Lola – The Illustrated History (1957-1977) (Starkey)
Lola – All The Sports Racing & Single-seater Racing Cars 1978-1997 (Starkey)
Lola T70 – The Racing History & Individual Chassis Record 4th Edition (Starkey)
Lotus 49 (Oliver)
Marketingmobiles, The Wonderful Wacky World Of (Hale)
Mazda MX-5/Miata 1.6 Enthusiast's Workshop Manual (Grainger & Shoemark)
Mazda MX-5/Miata 1.8 Enthusiast's Workshop Manual (Grainger & Shoemark)
Mazda MX-5 Miata: The Book Of The World's Favourite Sportscar (Long)
Mazda MX-5 Miata Roadster (Long)
MGA (Price Williams)
MGB & MGB GT– Expert Guide (Auto-doc Series) (Williams)
MGB Electrical Systems (Astley)
Micro Caravans (Jenkinson)
Micro Trucks (Mort)
Microcars At Large! (Quellin)
Mini Cooper – The Real Thing! (Tipler)
Mitsubishi Lancer Evo, The Road Car & WRC Story (Long)
Montlhéry, The Story Of The Paris Autodrome (Boddy)
Morgan Maverick (Lawrence)
Morris Minor, 60 Years On The Road (Newell)
Moto Guzzi Sport & Le Mans Bible (Falloon)
Motor Movies – The Posters! (Veysey)
Motor Racing – Reflections Of A Lost Era (Carter)
Motorcycle Apprentice (Cakebread)
Motorcycle Road & Racing Chassis Designs (Noakes)
Motorhomes, The Illustrated History (Jenkinson)
Motorsport In colour, 1950s (Wainwright)
Nissan 300ZX & 350Z – The Z-Car Story (Long)
Off-Road Giants! – Heroes of 1960s Motorcycle Sport (Westlake)
Pass The Theory And Practical Driving Tests (Gibson & Hoole)
Peking To Paris 2007 (Young)
Plastic Toy Cars Of The 1950s & 1960s (Ralston)
Pontiac Firebird (Cranswick)
Porsche Boxster (Long)
Porsche 964, 993 & 996 Data Plate Code Breaker (Streather)
Porsche 356 (2nd Edition) (Long)
Porsche 911 Carrera – The Last Of The Evolution (Corlett)
Porsche 911R, RS & RSR, 4th Edition (Starkey)
Porsche 911 – The Definitive History 1963-1971 (Long)
Porsche 911 – The Definitive History 1971-1977 (Long)
Porsche 911 – The Definitive History 1977-1987 (Long)
Porsche 911 – The Definitive History 1987-1997 (Long)
Porsche 911 – The Definitive History 1997-2004 (Long)
Porsche 911SC 'Super Carrera' – The Essential Companion (Streather)
Porsche 914 & 914-6: The Definitive History Of The Road & Competition Cars (Long)
Porsche 924 (Long)
Porsche 944 (Long)
Porsche 993 'King Of Porsche' – The Essential Companion (Streather)
Porsche 996 'Supreme Porsche' – The Essential Companion (Streather)
Porsche Racing Cars – 1953 To 1975 (Long)
Porsche Racing Cars – 1976 On (Long)
Porsche – The Rally Story (Meredith)
Porsche: Three Generations Of Genius (Meredith)
RAC Rally Action! (Gardiner)
Rallye Sport Fords: The Inside Story (Moreton)
Redman, Jim – 6 Times World Motorcycle Champion: The Autobiography (Redman)
Rolls-Royce Silver Shadow/Bentley T Series Corniche & Camargue Revised & Enlarged Edition (Bobbitt)
Rolls-Royce Silver Spirit, Silver Spur & Bentley Mulsanne 2nd Edition (Bobbitt)
RX-7 – Mazda's Rotary Engine Sportscar (Updated & Revised New Edition) (Long)
Scooters & Microcars, The A-Z Of Popular (Dan)
Scooter Lifestyle (Grainger)
Singer Story: Cars, Commercial Vehicles, Bicycles & Motorcycles (Atkinson)
SM – Citroën's Maserati-engined Supercar (Long & Claverol)
Subaru Impreza: The Road Car And WRC Story (Long)
Taxi! The Story Of The 'London' Taxicab (Bobbitt)
Tinplate Toy Cars Of The 1950s & 1960s (Ralston)
Toyota Celica & Supra, The Book Of Toyota's Sports Coupés (Long)
Toyota MR2 Coupés & Spyders (Long)
Triumph Motorcycles & The Meriden Factory (Hancox)
Triumph Speed Twin & Thunderbird Bible (Woolridge)
Triumph Tiger Cub Bible (Estall)
Triumph Trophy Bible (Woolridge)
Triumph TR6 (Kimberley)
Unraced (Collins)
Velocette Motorcycles – MSS To Thruxton Updated & Revised (Burris)
Virgil Exner – Visioneer: The Official Biography Of Virgil M Exner Designer Extraordinaire (Grist)
Volkswagen Bus Book, The (Bobbitt)
Volkswagen Bus Or Van To Camper, How To Convert (Porter)
Volkswagens Of The World (Glen)
VW Beetle Cabriolet (Bobbitt)
VW Beetle – The Car Of The 20th Century (Copping)
VW Bus – 40 Years Of Splitties, Bays & Wedges (Copping)
VW Bus Book, The (Bobbitt)
VW Golf: Five Generations Of Fun (Copping & Cservenka)
VW – The Air-cooled Era (Copping)
VW T5 Camper Conversion Manual (Porter)
VW Campers (Copping)
Works Minis, The Last (Purves & Brenchley)
Works Rally Mechanic (Moylan)

www.veloce.co.uk

First published in July 2008 by Veloce Publishing Limited, 33 Trinity Street, Dorchester DT1 1TT, England. Fax 01305 268864/e-mail info@veloce.co.uk/web www.veloce.co.uk or www.velocebooks.com.
ISBN: 978-1-84584-163-8/UPC: 6-36847-04163-2

Readers with ideas for automotive books, or books on other transport or related hobby subjects, are invited to write to the editorial director of Veloce Publishing at the above address.
British Library Cataloguing in Publication Data - A catalogue record for this book is available from the British Library. Typesetting, design and page make-up all by Veloce Publishing Ltd on Apple Mac.
Printed in India by Replika Press.

Introduction & thanks
– the purpose of this book

The Subaru Impreza began life as one of the world's best-kept secrets, but quickly became a performance car legend and a rally icon. This book aims to simplify the process of buying one of these superb cars, from the earliest official imports to the third generation editions that ran until 2007 when Subaru introduced the radically altered hatchback version.

Subaru initially launched the Impreza to its domestic Japanese market in 1992 as a direct replacement for the L-Series. The company was the first to introduce all-wheel drive cars as everyday vehicles rather than off-roaders, and the Impreza was a continuation of that thinking. What Subaru hadn't counted on was how much of an impact this new car would make. Central to the range was the turbo edition and its EJ20 flat-four engine which would seal the car's cult status among motoring aficionados, and while the car has since been refined and restyled, Subaru has essentially built its continued success on this base model.

The Impreza Turbo 2000: the car that began it all for the UK in 1994.

There are plenty of Imprezas available, from the original 'classics' (1992-2000) to the second (2000-2002) and third generation models (2002-2007). With such a large range, there is an Impreza to suit most pockets, and this book aims to assist in finding the right car for the right price.

It is worth stressing the importance of being thorough when buying an Impreza; although the words 'full Subaru service history' are perhaps not as sexy as the World Rally Blue paintwork that's gleaming at you, it is vital to check the mechanics and the history

GB270: the last special edition before Subaru completely changed the style and direction of the Impreza.
(Courtesy Subaru (UK) Ltd)

of the car. These are performance vehicles that are likely to have been driven with performance in mind; subsequently, they ought to have received the corresponding level of care and attention to keep them working. If you have doubts about a car's history or the seller's honesty, walk away from the purchase – there are plenty of others to choose from out there.

Within the standard WRX and STi ranges is a large minority special editions such as the WRX WRP10, Terzo, RB5 and P1. Some of these limited editions have acquired a certain caché among enthusiasts, reflected in the slightly higher-than-average second-hand prices. To some extent, this book will incorporate these models into the overall buying experience, but, for conciseness, much of what is written will relate to the original equipment manufacturer (OEM) versions. For more detailed information on limited editions contact the relevant owners groups, where enthusiasm and knowledge run deep, take a look at the excellent Impreza Web Owner's Club website (www.iwoc.co.uk), or consult *Subaru Impreza: The Road Car & WRC Story* by Brian Long (Veloce Publishing).

Thanks

I have had the pleasure of owning an Impreza Turbo 2000 for ten years, and during that time have tested many others.

Ownership has been complemented through membership of the Subaru Impreza Driver's Club where support has been readily available, especially during my time as editor of the club magazine; my appreciation goes to the many members who have offered advice and provided information, and I would specifically like to thank John Stewart and Craig Mudd, who ensured I stayed pointing in the right direction.

Thanks also go to Arthur Fairley and Kate Bishop at Subaru (UK) Ltd, Dave Kosbab and all the staff at Cheam Motors in Surrey, and Graham Cowland at TSL-Motorsport in Nottinghamshire for their time and knowledge.

David Hobbs

The 2005 WRX STi Type UK at launch. (Courtesy Subaru (UK) Ltd)

Contents

1 Is it the right car for you?
– marriage guidance

Tall and short drivers
Most drivers can be accommodated. Height-adjustable seats also have good forward and backward range.

Weight of controls
Power steering more precise as Subaru developed the chassis. Improved short-throw gearshifts replaced long-throw levers. Although on the heavy side, clutch should pose no problem.

Will it fit in the garage?
Dimensions of largest Impreza (2007 2.5WRX/STi):
Length – 4465mm
Width – 1740mm (saloon), 1695mm (estate)

Interior space
Five adults comfortably accommodated. More boot space in the estates with seats folded. Some saloons' back seats do not fold. Boot space limited if a rear strut brace fitted.

The 2003 revamped WRX that saved the Impreza. (Courtesy Subaru (UK) Ltd)

Running costs
Six-month or 7500 mile service for early models, but now annual or 10,000 miles. Oil change every 5000 miles recommended. Official combined fuel consumption for the latest 2.5 WRX STi is 25.9mpg, but this figure drops with hard use.

Useability
Equally at home on twisty country roads and in urban traffic.

Parts availability
Generally excellent, and that includes the first models.

Parts cost
On the whole, service and parts costs are high. Discounts are available through enthusiast organisations.

Insurance
High, typically group 17-20 in the UK.

Investment potential
All models are still depreciating, including popular limited editions.

Plus points
The Impreza is a superb performance car and any model will have unbelievable power, grip and handling.

Minus points
Target for thieves. Cheap, boy-racer image has developed. Fuel costs can be crippling.

Alternatives
Mitsubishi Lancer Evo, Audi S4, Ford Focus RS, Ford Focus ST, Honda Civic Type R, BMW 330i M Sport.

2 Cost considerations
– affordable, or a money pit?

Running costs can be high, starting with insurance and fuel.
Service periods –
Turbo 2000: 7500 miles (12,500km) or six months
WRX/STi: 12,000 miles (19,000km) or annual for 2.0-litre cars
and 10,000 miles (16,000km) for 2.5-litre models.

Typical costs based on a model year 2003 (MY03) WRX –
Small service: ●x182
Large service: ●x497
New clutch (fitted): ●x822
Brake disc (each): ●x59 (front), ●x53 (rear)
Brake pads: ●x102 (front), ●x50 (rear)
New wing: ●x86
New headlight: ●x237
4x17-inch Prodrive Speedline alloy wheels: ●x700
Air filter: ●x15
Timing belt: ●x80 (for 45,000-mile service)
Driver's airbag: ●x857
Passenger's airbag: ●x947
Tyres (each): ●x100-plus
ECU: ●x825

The 2006 WRX 2.5L engine will need care and attention. (Courtesy Subaru (UK) Ltd)

Used parts
Readily available from dismantlers and enthusiasts' clubs.

17in alloy wheel and Bridgestone tyre of 2006 WRX STi Type UK.

Driver's side front headlight of 2006 WRX STi Type UK.

Good points

If you're looking for a performance car with impeccable motorsport heritage and a unique look, then the Impreza could be the answer.

These are cars guaranteed to bring a smile to your face, and considering the performance levels into which you are buying, they are a relative bargain. Whichever model you purchase you'll find they make driving a real thrill, with superb acceleration and torque characteristics matched by unbelievable handling capabilities – you'll just stick to the road like glue.

With six World Rally Championships to its name, the Impreza enjoys a rich heritage and still earns respect in the motorsport and performance car worlds, even when faced with new pretenders and the challenges they bring.

It's not all about flinging the car around twisty roads though; the versatile Impreza is a more-than capable daily driver, and can sit in heavy traffic quite comfortably without straining at the leash. The model's reputation for reliability and build quality was backed up by its number one position in the UK-based JD Power customer satisfaction survey for two years running.

The estate version (Turbo and WRX

Numerous rally titles around the world have made the Impreza the rally car of choice for many competitors.

The five-door Impreza has equal performance levels to the Saloon – but with a little more practicality. (Courtesy Subaru (UK) Ltd)

only) also offers the choice of a more practical family car without sacrificing any of the performance. Overall, the range of models is broad enough to enable buyers to choose one that suits their lifestyle, whether they are looking for a high-spec WRX STi or a standard Turbo 2000 estate.

The engines will enjoy a long life if well looked after; running costs on newer models have dropped slightly thanks to longer service intervals. All new Imprezas now come with a three-year or 60,000-mile warranty, three-year paintwork guarantee and 12-year anti-corrosion warranty.

There is a large body of enthusiasts that makes up an active community offering information, advice, social events, track days and more to owners. All are passionate about the Impreza and offer a warm welcome to like-minded people. This community is backed up by an extensive network of official and independent

Driving comfort has improved, as the interior of the GB270 illustrates. (Courtesy Subaru (UK) Ltd)

dealers who are equally as enthusiastic about the car and extracting the best performance from it. If you're looking to modify an Impreza with either official or unofficial upgrades, then these people or the club members are the ones to talk to.

Bad points

Running costs are not cheap. OK, they stand up to comparison with their rivals, but remember that driving an Impreza away from the dealer is only the first dent in your wallet ...

Because the Impreza has become a favourite target for thieves, insurance costs have risen dramatically; in the UK, the model is in groups 19 and 20. There are specialist insurers and brokers available, so it's worth shopping around for quotations. In the UK, the Impreza is also in a high road-tax bracket. Service intervals have been extended, but even so, regular servicing is essential to keep the Impreza in top condition. Any skimping may come back to haunt you, and could even affect resale value.

Bodywork is well looked after, thanks to a 12-year anti-corrosion warranty.

The Impreza is a thirsty beast (minimum 97RON fuel is recommended), so expect frequent visits to the fuel pumps. If the car is to be used as a daily commuter, costs can quickly mount up. Although you can squeeze 30mpg out of the engine, expect a much lower average figure, especially with some 'spirited' driving or track days, which will see fuel consumption rocket.

Road noise can be intrusive; driving around town causes no real problems, but at high motorway speeds the noise can become annoying, especially with low profile tyres fitted – the poor stereo system will not resolve the problem either.

Interiors, particularly among the original classics, are uninspiring and look dated, but they have improved over the years and now offer a pretty good package. But don't get too hung up about what's inside the car, otherwise you'll be missing the point; drive an Impreza how it's meant to be driven, and you'll be too busy enjoying what's going on outside to bother questioning the colour coding inside the cabin.

With such stunning performance comes temptation, but with the relentless rise of the Gatso camera in the UK, penalty points on your licence or worse are a real possibility. Track days can help satisfy a thirst for speed – just make sure any warranty is not affected.

In spite of the rally heritage, the Impreza is developing an image problem, often being perceived as a car for the boy-racer fraternity. With the early models now readily available for little money, poorly maintained, tired examples are becoming more common, which takes away some of the shine.

4 Relative values
– which model for you?

Here for your guidance, and as a percentage of the original retail price (see chapter 17), are the relative values of individual models (2.0-litre turbos unless otherwise stated) as at the time of writing, but please double-check with local price guides. Popular limited editions are also listed.

First Generation (Japan)

WRX saloon, WRX RA, WRX SA (1994 only): 1992-94 237bhp (240ps); 1994-96 256bhp (260ps); 1996-2000 276bhp (280ps) 10-24%

WRX Sports Wagon: 1993-96 216bhp (220ps); 1996-2000 237-246bhp (240-250ps) 10-24%

WRX STi: 1994-1995 246bhp (250ps); Version II 1995-96 271bhp (275ps); Version II Sports Wagon 256bhp (260ps); 1996-2000 Version III-VI 276bhp (280ps) 10-25%

WRX STi RA: 1994-2000 (275ps) 10-30%·

WRX STi Type R (two-door coupe): 1997-2000 276bhp (280ps) 10-25%

Limited editons: Type R 22B 276bhp (280ps); STi S201 295bhp (300ps) 40-50%

First Generation (Australia, Europe)

Turbo 2000 (UK), WRX (Australia), GT (Europe): 1994-96 208bhp (211ps) 12-16%; 1996-2000 215bhp (218ps) 16-24%; Prodrive Performance Pack/ WR Sport 1996-2000 238bhp (240ps) 15-20%

WRX STi Version VI (Australia): 2000 276bhp (280ps) 15-25%

Limited editions: Series McRae, Catalunya, Terzo, RB5/RB5 PPP 208/238bhp (211/240ps) 8-23%; 22B Type UK 276bhp (280ps) 40-50%; P1 276bhp (280ps) 20-30%; Club Spec,

The Impreza Catalunya was released in 1997 to celebrate Subaru's second successive WRC manufacturers' title. (Courtesy Subaru (UK) Ltd)

22B: the Holy Grail for many Impreza enthusiasts, and still highly sought-after. (Courtesy Subaru (UK) Ltd)

With the Prodrive extras, the RB5 became one of the most revered among the limited editions. (Courtesy Mark Chamberlain/RB5 Owner's Club)

Club Spec Evo 2-4 215bhp (218ps)
16-24%

Second Generation Impreza (Japan)
WRX/20K/Sports Wagon: 2000-07
247bhp (250ps) 25-80%
WRX STi: 2000-05 276bhp (280ps);
2000-01 STi Wagon 256bhp (260ps);
2006-07 276bhp (280ps) 30-80%
WRX STi Type RA, Type RA Spec C:
276bhp (280ps) 30-80%
Limited editions: S202, S203, S204
316bhp (320ps); WRX STi Spec C
V-Limited 276bhp (280ps); WRX STi
Spec C Type RA-R 2007 320bhp
(324ps) 30-90%

Second Generation Impreza (Australia, Europe)
WRX: 2000-02 215bhp (218ps), PPP
242bhp (245ps) 24-30%;
WRX/WRX SL: 2003-05 222bhp
(225ps), PPP 261bhp (265ps) 40-50%;
2006-07 2.5 litre engine introduced
226bhp (230ps) 60-70%
WRX STi: 2002 261 bhp (265ps)
(Australia) 20-25%
WRX STi: 2002-05 261bhp (265ps),
PPP 300bhp (305ps) 30-55%; 2006-07
2.5 litre engine introduced WRX STi/STi
Spec D 277bhp (281ps) 60-70%
Limited editions: UK 300/UK 300 PPP
215/241bhp (218/245ps) 25-30%; WR1
316bhp (320ps) 45-55%; RB320 316bhp
(320ps) 65-70%; GB270 266bhp (270ps)
75%; WRX Club Spec Evo 5-8, WRX
Club Spec 9 222bhp (225ps) 40-80%;
WRX WRP10 235bhp (238ps) 55-65%

Second Generation Impreza (USA)
WRX/WRX Premium: 2002-05 227bhp
(230ps) 25-40%
WRX, WRX TR (Tuner Ready), Limited:
2006-07 2.5 litre engine introduced 224bhp (227ps)
50-80%
WRX STi/STI/STI Limited: 2004-07 2.5
litre engine 293bhp (297ps) 40-80%

The launch of the second
generation Impreza in 2000 met
with a decidedly mixed reception.
(Courtesy Subaru (UK) Ltd)

The limited edition WR1 was released to
mark Petter Solberg's 2003 WRC title.
(Courtesy Subaru (UK) Ltd)

The 2006 WRX and STi models
introduced the 2.5-litre engines
to the UK market.

5 Before you view
– be well informed

To avoid the frustration of a car not meeting your expectations, remember to ask specific questions when you call *before* viewing. Also, check the current values of the model you are interested in in the car magazines that feature price guides, or the price guide booklets available to the public.

Where is the car?
Is it going to be worth travelling to view the car? A locally advertised car, although it might not sound very interesting, can add to your knowledge for very little effort, so make a visit: it might even be in better condition than expected.

Dealer or private sale?
Establish early on if the car is being sold by its owner or by a trader. A private owner should have all the history. A dealer may have more limited knowledge of a car's history, but should have some documentation. A dealer may offer a warranty/guarantee (ask for a printed copy), and finance.

Cost of collection and delivery?
A dealer may well be used to quoting for delivery by car transporter. A private owner may agree to meet you halfway, but only agree to this after you have seen the car at the vendor's address to validate the documents. You could meet halfway and agree the sale, but insist on meeting at the vendor's address for the handover.

View: when and where?
It is always preferable to view at the vendor's home or business premises. In the case of a private sale, the car's documentation should tally with the vendor's name and address. Arrange to view only in daylight and avoid a wet day. Most cars look better in poor light or when wet.

Reason for sale?
Do make it one of the first questions. Why is the car being sold and how long has it been with the current owner? How many previous owners?

Conversions?
Cars that have been customised or have larger engines fitted must be given special consideration as to the competency of the conversion.

Condition (body/chassis/interior/mechanicals)?
Ask for an honest appraisal of the car's condition. Ask specifically about some of the check items described in chapter 7.

All original specification?
An original equipment car is invariably of higher value than a customised version.

Matching data/legal ownership?

Do VIN/chassis, engine numbers and licence plate match the official registration document? Is the owner's name and address recorded in the official registration documents? For those countries that require an annual test of roadworthiness, does the car have a document showing it complies (an MoT certificate in the UK, which can be verified on 0845 600 5977)?

If a smog/emissions certificate is mandatory, does the car have one? If required, does the car carry a current road fund licence/licence plate tag?

Does the vendor own the car outright? Money might be owed to a finance company or bank: the car could even be stolen. Several organisations, for a fee, will supply the ownership data, based on the car's licence plate number. Such companies can often also tell you whether the car has been 'written off' by an insurance company. These organisations can supply vehicle data –

HPI	01722 422 422 (UK)
AA	0870 600 0836 (UK)
DVLA	0870 240 0010 (UK)
RAC	0870 533 3660 (UK)
Carfax	http://www.carfax.com (USA)
Autocheck	http://www.autocheck.com (USA)

Other countries will have similar organisations.

Insurance?

Check with your existing insurer before setting out, as your current policy might not cover you to drive the car if you do purchase it.

How you can pay

A cheque/check will take several days to clear and the seller may prefer to sell to a cash buyer. However, a banker's draft (a cheque issued by a bank) is as good as cash, but safer, so contact your own bank and become familiar with the formalities that are necessary to obtain one.

Buying at auction?

If the intention is to buy at auction, see chapter 10 for further advice.

Professional vehicle check (mechanical examination)

There are often marque/model specialists who will undertake professional examination of a vehicle on your behalf. Owners clubs will be able to put you in touch with such specialists. Other organisations that will carry out a general professional include –

AA	0800 085 3007 (UK motoring organisation with vehicle inspectors)
ABS	0800 358 5855 (UK specialist vehicle inspection company)
RAC	0870 533 3660 (UK motoring organisation with vehicle inspectors)
AAA	http://www.aaa.com (USA motoring organisation with vehicle inspection centres)

Other countries will have similar organisations.

6 Inspection equipment
– these items will really help

Before you rush out of the door, gather together a few items that will help as you work around the car.

This book
This book is designed to be your guide at every step, so take it along and use the check boxes to help you assess each area of the car you're interested in. Don't be afraid to let the seller see you using it.

Glasses (spectacles)
Take your reading glasses if you need them, to read documents and make close-up inspections.

Magnet (not powerful, a fridge magnet is ideal)
A magnet will help you check if the car is full of filler, or has fibreglass panels. Use the magnet to sample bodywork areas all around the car, but be careful not to damage the paintwork. Expect to find a little filler here and there, but not whole panels. There's nothing wrong with fibreglass panels, but a purist might want the car to be as original as possible.

Torch
A torch with fresh batteries will be useful for peering into the wheelarches and under the car.

Probe or small screwdriver
A small screwdriver can be used – with care – as a probe, particularly in the wheelarches and on the underside. With this you should be able to check an area of severe corrosion, but be careful – if it's really bad the screwdriver might go through the metal!

Overalls
Be prepared to get dirty. Take along a pair of overalls if you have them.

Mirror on a stick
Fixing a mirror at an angle on the end of a stick may seem odd, but you'll probably need it to check the condition of the underside of the car. It will also help you to peer into some of the important crevices. You can also use it, together with the torch, along the underside of the sills and on the floor.

Digital camera
If you have the use of a digital camera, take it along so that later you can study some areas of the car more closely at your leisure. Take a picture of any part of the car that causes you concern, and seek a knowledgeable friend's opinion. Ideally, have a friend or knowledgeable enthusiast accompany you: a second opinion is always valuable.

Exterior

With a plentiful supply of enthusiasts running Imprezas there should be little problem in finding one that has been well maintained, so a first glance ought to provide a strong indication as to a car's purchase potential.

Solidly built and made to last, Imprezas are robust, but that does not make them immune to damage. On first examination check that the paintwork is glossy and consistent; any

An immaculate 2006 Impreza WRX STi.

irregularities may reflect some level of repair work, a poor respray, or both, so check the paperwork. Stone chips on the bumper and bonnet are common.

On the whole, there should be little or no evidence of rust; all UK cars, for instance, were undersealed and came with a six-year anti-corrosion warranty (later models were given 12-year cover). However, some of the first Imprezas are now beyond corrosion guarantee, so there may be signs of rust. These could include

Stone chips are common on the front bumper, but other damage will need further investigation.

MY 2006 rear light cluster with STi badging.

the bumper attachment points and some areas in the engine bay, particularly if the car has not been garaged. If there is rust here, look underneath the car thoroughly for any further signs, but note that any you find is likely to be superficial, and it is uncommon to see rust in any structural area.

If you find an older example with no stone chips, check the documents, or simply ask if the owner has had the car resprayed or the bonnet refurbished. If no paperwork is forthcoming, be wary – the car may be concealing more serious damage repairs.

Rust may be more of a concern on Japanese market vehicles that have not been undersealed, and are therefore susceptible to the effects of the salt used to clear icy roads. If buying one, make sure adequate precautions have been taken to protect the car and undertake a close examination underneath.

Check for any odd or excessive panel gaps, overspray on other areas of the bodywork and any marks under the paintwork. If there are obvious signs of repair then make sure the documentation matches the explanation. If in doubt, walk away.

Some models such as the P1 came with different body kit, but you will find many that have been altered – side skirts, front and rear bumpers, lightweight aluminium bonnets and rear spoilers are all common modifications; ensure they have been securely and properly fitted.

Look underneath the car on the undertray, and also on the

bottom of the front bumper; deep marks and scrapes may have been caused by off-road and/or hard road driving. Closer checks will be needed to determine if more serious damage has been inflicted.

The drab 15in alloy wheels on the 1992-97 turbos have probably been upgraded to 16 or 17in versions; some of these early wheels were found to be porous, resulting in loss of tyre pressure, but any such affected wheels are likely to have been long since replaced. From 1997, the wheels were upgraded to 16in and then to 17in from 2001. Examine the wheels for scratches and signs of kerbing.

Like many performance cars, the tyres are going to take some punishment if driven hard. Rubber can last for around 20,000 miles, but much less if driven hard, and front tyres wear more quickly than rear ones; many owners swap the front and rear tyres every six months to even out tyre wear. If the seller has records of the number of tyres changes made it will give a better insight into how the car has been driven, rather than how far. Uneven tyre wear may signify a few problems – the wheels are not aligned correctly, the car has regularly been driven hard, some suspension components may be bent or worn, or the body has been damaged at some point and not correctly repaired.

Front and rear lamps are popular targets for modifications, especially on the classic turbos which had notoriously weak headlights. Similarly, the second generation cars underwent the same treatment in order to remove the unloved 'Bugeye' look. The important thing here is to check that the wiring has been upgraded with an auxiliary loom, because the standard wiring could not cope with bigger headlights.

There should be a Subaru Seven Stars badge on the front grille on all Imprezas. Japanese first generation STis show a pink 'S' badge, but all UK cars were fitted with the seven stars. However, the pink badges were popular and may have been fitted to non-STi versions. There ought to be an 'STi'-lettered badge on the right of the boot, as well as 'WRX Impreza' on the left. Because these badges can be bought from aftermarket suppliers it is essential to check the car is actually what it claims to be. The easiest way to do this is by matching the model number (located in the engine bay) with the vehicle's documentation.

Interior
In the early days, Subaru was not overly concerned with the Impreza's interior – and it showed. In standard form, classic versions will be furnished with dull, grey cloth and plastic, the latter being particularly prone to scratching so expect to see some marks on the older models. Seats were little more than adequate and many owners will have replaced them for the more supportive Recaros. If the originals are still in place, look for wear and tear and any sagging. Similarly, check the footwell carpets, door trims, gear knobs, pedals and seatbelt tension. The pre-1996 models may look

Early Impreza Turbo interiors were bland and uninspiring.

dated (or 'classic', depending on your point of view) and will reflect their age, but should not be scruffy if properly cared for.

Improvements continued throughout the Impreza's life cycle and in 1998 the interior was given a major overhaul. More robust, it included a new dashboard featuring white dials, a computerised odometer and a low fuel light as well as sports seats as standard. A passenger airbag, Momo leather steering wheel, leather-covered handbrake lever and a shorter throw gear lever completed the update.

From 2000, the second and third generation cars have enjoyed closer attention in terms of comfort and styling, so expect some variation if looking at different model years; for example, from 2003 the STi sported blue suede-effect Alcantara seats with STi stitched in to the backs, as well as red stitching on the Momo steering wheel, six-speed gear knob and handbrake.

One of the key selling points for the limited editions such as the RB5 and Catalunya were the superior interior trims. Because of their rarity, well-maintained examples are always worth a look, and probably worth the higher premium if the rest of the car matches up.

As well as the front seats, the low quality stereo systems are usually the first items to be thrown out and replaced with superior versions. Also expect to find different steering wheels, gear knobs and an array of gauges on the dash or the pillar. These are often all for the better but make sure they have been properly installed, especially if done by owners. Replacing the steering wheel on some models involves disabling the airbag, and this may have insurance implications.

The spare wheel, jack handle and tools will be located under the carpet in the boot, with the jack found in a side pocket on the boot's left wall.

Paperwork/ownership/legality

One point to stress more than any other in the buying process is the necessity for a full Subaru service history (FSSH). This crucial documentation is the reassurance that proves the car has received the necessary mechanical examination at the requisite times. Examine the service book and receipts to ensure that servicing has been maintained. Predictably, the service costs will increase throughout the car's life, with timing belts a particularly costly exercise. These are changed every three years or after 45,000 miles, so look to see if this service is imminent.

Checking VIN plates and paperwork is vitally important.

The car's vehicle identification number (VIN) is stamped onto a plate located in the engine bay. The plate also displays the model code, paint code and trim code. Make sure the VIN number displayed matches the number on the registration document and that the car is the right model you are looking at (for more on these codes, see chapter 17).

When buying an Impreza from an official Subaru dealer you can have more confidence in the car's history. If less than three years old, the car will still be under warranty, unless unapproved modifications have been carried out. Once that period has passed, the 'Subaru proven used cars' scheme carries certain guarantees, including an extendable 12-month warranty, confirmation the car has not been stolen, written off or is still subject to outstanding finance and a vehicle mileage check certificate.

Mechanicals

If you're happy with what you've seen so far then it's time to look under the bonnet/hood and start the engine.

Open the bonnet (the catch is underneath the dash on the driver's side), and you should be met with a clean engine bay with no fluid leaks. These have not been a problem for the Impreza, so any signs of leaking may point to an engine that has been taken apart and badly put back together. Using the dipstick, check the oil – it should be slightly coloured and smooth if rubbed

A well-maintained engine is key to successful Impreza ownership.

on your fingers. If the oil is black it hasn't been changed recently. Check the receipts to make sure that a high quality, fully synthetic oil has been used, noting that some modern, low viscosity oils are outside the recommended range for the engine.

Look to see if the fins on the intercooler are upright and not bent. If many are damaged or blocked by debris, the intercooler's performance can be seriously hampered.

The boxer engine that has been the mainstay of the Impreza throughout the model's life is reliable, tuneable and quick. However, to keep it in tip-top working condition, correct servicing by Subaru dealers or reputable specialists is essential. After you have started the car (preferably from cold) there ought to be a satisfyingly off-beat and throaty rumble from the flat-four boxer engine. If that is all you hear, then things are looking up.

Things to look out for immediately include a loud ticking or 'slapping' noise, particularly on 1997 and 1998 models. Piston slap was a common problem on these cars and most were fixed under warranty; check the service history to see if this was done. If the sound is coming from an earlier model then the pistons may be failing, and it would be worth getting expert advice. These are not cheap to fix so if the noise continues once the car is up to operating temperatures, negotiate a price reduction. You don't want to be paying thousands on an engine rebuild later if the pistons fail.

Rev the engine and let it return to idle. If you hear a rattle from the engine then the rod bearing or big end might need replacing. Again insist on a healthy discount to sort it out, or, better still, find another car.

When revving the Impreza's engine, also watch for any blue or white smoke from the exhaust. If blue smoke persists, there is a problem with the engine. Similarly, white smoke (not to be confused with steam) when the engine is cold is a sign of turbocharger problems. Listen for any excessive whining from the turbo, as well as a 'mooing' sound which could mean a dodgy dump valve.

Original twin-pipe exhausts on the classic models are rare.

Blocked and bent fins can reduce the effectiveness of the Impreza's intercooler.

Turbos are victims of some abuse from owners who may not be prepared to spare a little time over their care. If your seller demonstrates the car, see how they treat the engine from cold – it should be given time to warm up before any serious throttle is applied above 3000rpm, and again at the end of any journey the turbo must be allowed to cool down. This can be done by either gentle driving for the last mile or so or by letting the engine idle for a few minutes. If the owner does neither then be very wary.

Many Imprezas will have had their exhaust systems modified. This may only be a new backbox but listen to the noise and be certain it is something with which you (and your neighbours!) can live. More extensive modifications can involve removing the catalytic converters. However, these are required to pass MoT tests, so make sure the owner still has them if they are not fitted.

Check the front and rear lamps; these are popular areas for modifying, especially on the 2000-02 models, to remove the 'bugeye' look as well as the rear clusters. Ensure they have been fitted properly and that they are legal.

Check the controls inside the cabin to make sure they are all working. The Impreza's electronics have always been reliable, and it is generally only aftermarket modifications that prove problematic, such as the poor headlamp upgrades mentioned above. Give the air-conditioning a good workout to make sure the system is fully operational (it is recommended you let the air-con run for a few minutes each month) by switching from cold to hot settings. The system should respond quickly.

The Impreza's transmission has a solid reputation, with improvements from 2000 onwards. If the clutch's biting point is high, then the clutch may need replacing soon. Clutch judder is a common issue when moving off with a cold engine, but does not necessarily signify problems. However, if the judder continues when the car is warmed up then again the clutch may need changing. As this is an expensive job, particularly if a new flywheel is required, it will be worth a closer examination before purchase.

The engine is controlled by an electronic system known as the ECU. A quick way to check it is working is by listening to the engine. If the engine idles at high revs when at normal operating temperatures then something may be wrong, and will need further investigation. Re-mapping of Imprezas is a common modification, so again make sure any ECU changes have been carried out by a reputable and qualified technician.

Gear changes ought to be smooth and crisp, although on some models (such as the STi from 2002 onwards) the gears may feel notchy. These shifts were given extra rigidity to withstand the high torque outputs from the six-speed gearboxes. On all models, though, there should be no whining from the gearbox. If there is and it increases when accelerating, then the bearings may need changing.

8 Key points

– where to look for problems

There are five areas to bear in mind:

Bodywork

Check for uneven paintwork concealing badly repaired accident damage or poor colour matching from stone chip paint renovation. Look for uneven or excessive panel gaps. There should be no signs of rust or corrosion. Tyre tread wear must be even, while wheels should show few signs of kerbing or other damage. Aftermarket headlights and rear lamps need wiring upgrades.

Interior

The interiors of early models were dull but should still be in good condition. Later models have superior and more robust interiors. Check for sagging in front seats and signs of excess wear on gearshift and pedals. Ensure any non-standard stereo systems and gauges have been properly fitted.

Service history

A full Subaru service history is essential – the more paperwork, receipts, etc., the better.

Engine

The engine bay should be clean and rust-free with no fluid leaks. Check the intercooler fins are in good condition.

Underbody

Look underneath the front bumper for damage that could have been caused by hard off-road driving. Check the undertray and exhaust pipe for similar signs of abuse. Examine the suspension arms to make sure they are not bent or scratched.

2006 WRX STi – bodywork should be perfect.

Kerbing damage is not unusual, but should not be excessive.

Wear ought to be even on all four tyres.

Impreza interiors have improved, as this GB270 illustrates.

A view of the rear wheel with suspension arms.

Original older Impreza seats may be tired – check closely.

Exterior

A brief check of the car should give a pretty good indication of what to expect on closer examination. The vast majority of Imprezas have been sold to enthusiasts or the curious who then became enthusiasts. The result is that there are numerous examples available that are in excellent condition. If you are presented with a shabby, tired-looking Impreza then you may not have reached this far in the inspection. If you have, you might want to rethink.

Bodywork and panels

Ex   Gd   Av   Po

4   3   2   1

Begin at the front of the car as this is where stone chips are most often found. Damage will mostly be found on the bonnet (hood) and front bumper but the number of chips should not be excessive. Where there are chips, look closely and make sure the marks have not penetrated the paint completely, otherwise corrosion could develop. Make sure the bonnet scoop and the two small vents are not loose.

Open and check underneath the bonnet. On the whole, rust should not be apparent although this cannot be guaranteed on older models. While the bonnet is open check the engine bay is in sound condition.

Moving to the side of the car, door panels are thin and susceptible to those annoying car park 'dings'. Look at the panels from different angles to see if there are any small dents that show up in different light.

The roof can also suffer occasional stone chip damage, so look closely. The plastic runners along each side of the roof should be secure and not move

A quick all-over bodywork examination will give a good indication of condition.

Clean underside of MY06 WRX STi bonnet (hood) ...

... compared to the tired and rusting bonnet (hood) of a Turbo 2000.

The engine bay should be clean and leak-free.

excessively. Look into the 'gutters' where the runners are housed and check for any rust, as rain and dirt collect here. Open the boot (trunk) and check where the plastic runners meet the bodywork. Water can also collect here and if the area is not properly cared for and cleaned, rust will eventually set in. There are rubber plugs in the boot lid (trunk lid) to stop it rattling when shut – because they rub against the main bodywork the paint and primer will eventually wear away, and rust may develop.

Check the rear spoiler is secure; the larger STi spoilers will flex while those on the Turbo and WRX cars are more solid.

Examine the bumper attachment points and areas where extra bodykits may have been secured; these points are the most common areas for rust. Also ensure any bodykits have been securely fastened.

Body service

Ex	Gd	Av	Po
4	☑	2	1

As well as the regular engine servicing, Subaru also recommends bodywork servicing. The frequency and timing depends on the length of the anti-corrosion warranty; for example, on a MY95 Turbo the inspections were after one, three and five years. Each service follows the same format and ensures all areas have been treated with cavity wax. If areas have become dry or show signs of flaking, they need to be retreated. Particular attention is drawn to inside doors, bonnet, wheelarches, headlight area, box sections, boot-lid and door pillars while underneath the car all box sections and cavities need to be checked. If these services are not carried out the anti-corrosion warranty is invalidated. Check receipts and the service book for confirmation on any work undertaken.

Deep stone chips can cause problems if left.

One aspect of the anti-corrosion warranty to remember is that it applies to corrosion coming from the inside out. This means that stone chip damage that leads to rust is not covered, so look closely for deep chips because they will need treating if more serious damage at greater cost is to be avoided.

Paint

Ex	Gd	Av	Po
4	☑	2	1

The paint code for the car is located on the vehicle identification number (VIN), stamped onto a plate located in the engine bay. The colour will also be printed on the registration certificate (V5). If the code does not match the car, make sure you're happy with the reason for the difference. The colour should be consistent and glossy all over the car; any differences in shades or excessive paintwork may be concealing accident damage, so ask what repairs have been made. Another way to check for resprays is by looking in the spare wheel bay in the boot or underneath the doors; these are areas that may have been neglected in any 'dubious' respray.

Shut lines

Ex	Gd	Av	Po
☑	3	2	1

Because of the straightforward shape of the Impreza, it is easy to spot if the panels and shut lines are as they should be. Check the panel gaps are uniform.

The rubber seals on the windows ought to be clean, well-maintained and pressed

firmly against the window; if pockmarked and loose, they may need replacing. This is important to check because the Impreza's windows are frameless, so the seals are essential in keeping the rain out and the inside dry.

The bonnet should close flush and evenly. If not, check if the headlights have been replaced with aftermarket ones, particularly on the classic Imprezas. If badly fitted, they could have an effect on the bonnet's shut line.

The front and rear bumpers should have an evenly spaced gap with the main body. If not, check they are firmly attached. Similarly, check any bodykits have even lines with no large and unsightly gaps.

The shut lines on this rear door are not uniform and may signify poor repairs.

Exterior trim

A strip of plastic or rubber can sometimes be found down the side of the Impreza to protect the door panels. Just make sure it's properly fitted and secure, otherwise it can look cheap. The same goes for any other exterior trim or bodykit that has been added. Lower front bumpers and side skirts can make the Impreza look more aggressive and desirable, but with poor workmanship they can just appear tacky.

Wipers

The Impreza has two front wipers with three different speed and frequency settings, as well as a manual spray button that will simultaneously trigger the wiper blades. They should move smoothly across the glass with no juddering, otherwise they may need replacing. Not all models were fitted with a rear wiper, particularly the older classic editions, so don't expect to see one as standard.

Spoilers

Nearly all Impreza turbo variants come with a spoiler, the size and shape dependant on the model year and model type. The original saloon turbos came with a low-level rounded spoiler while the facelift sported a more upright version. With the launch of the New Age Imprezas, the flattened WRX spoilers were more akin to the first classics, albeit more stylised. Some spoilers may come fitted with additional rear brake lights. The latest saloon WRX models come without spoilers but can be fitted as optional extras.

The estate turbos wore their rear spoilers at the point where bodywork met rear window, but moved to the top of the rear windows when the new age WRX cars were introduced.

It is among the STi's and the limited edition Imprezas where the rally-style spoilers have more prominence. These have become more extreme as the cars have evolved – the first Type UK STi's offered a choice between the WRX and STi spoilers – and are a particularly striking visual characteristic of the Impreza. For those uncomfortable with such a large

The popular Prodrive spoiler: subtle it ain't. (Courtesy Subaru (UK) Ltd)

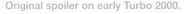
Original spoiler on early Turbo 2000.

rear end protrusion, the STi Spec D offers a more discreet version similar to the WRX. The latest STi also features an extra vane at the top of the rear window.

Of course, these are the standard spoilers, and owners may have replaced them with other aftermarket and extreme versions. If so, just check they are correctly fitted and that you can live with them.

The rear view from the driver's seat is not affected by Turbo and WRX spoilers; however, the larger types on the STi are clearly visible in the rear view mirror.

Rear vane added to STi with spoiler behind.

Lights

Ex Gd Av Po
☑ 3 2 1

The headlights are one of the most controversial developments on the Impreza. In the beginning came the rectangle-shaped headlights; however, these were not renowned for their strength and were hardly in keeping with the high performance values elsewhere on the car. They improved with the facelift

Headlight modifications on 'Bugeye' Imprezas improve the car's appearance.

classic, but even so, many were replaced with aftermarket sets, notably Morettes. These are a dramatic improvement and will make an Impreza more desirable. However, check they have been properly fitted and the wiring looms have been upgraded to take the extra power required.

The new generation cars brought with them the ovoid, or 'Bugeye' lights. These were met with a generally poor response, and in spite of Subaru's support for the new look, were soon replaced with the third generation 'teardrop' or 'blobeye' look. This has in turn developed into the 'hawkeye' appearance, sported on the 06-07 models. The power of the lights has improved and the Imprezas now carry HID headlamps.

The 'Hawkeye' headlights introduced in 2006 gave the Impreza an aggressive look not seen since the classic models.

Below the headlights are the front fog lamps, although these are not fitted to the STi as standard. Some owners may have changed the front fog lamps for extra driving lights.

Because of the negative feeling associated with the Bugeyes, many have been replaced to improve the car's appearance. However, there have been problems in terms of resilience and poor fitting – check closely.

Headlights and fog lamps of a facelift classic.

Right rear lamp cluster on a classic in good condition.

Questions need to be asked about how water got into this light unit.

Similarly, at the back there have been instances of damage to the seals if the rear lights have been removed (which was a popular modification among classic owners who thought the orange indicators unattractive). Water can leak through onto the boot floorpan, and possibly into the lights themselves. The expression 'de-tangoing' was coined to recognise when an owner had changed the rear, front and side indicators, usually for clear glass.

Glass

Ex	Gd	Av	Po
4	3	2	1

There are no reported problems with the Impreza's windows, but check for stone chips in the windscreen. The rear windshield is fitted with a de-mister.

Wheels and tyres

Ex	Gd	Av	Po
4	3	2	1

The Impreza's alloy wheels have improved since the days of the drab 15in wheels on the early Turbos. 1992-97 cars are likely to have been upgraded to 16 or 17in versions. However, if the original alloys are still present, check if they were repaired under warranty – some were slightly porous, resulting in loss of tyre pressure. From 1997, the wheels were upgraded to 16in and then to 17in from 2001. Gold wheels, standard on the STi, are popular and attract a higher premium. In 2005, the stud pattern for the wheels changed on the STi, moving 3-5mm closer together. As a result they cannot be transferred to earlier models.

Standard 10-spoke gold wheels on STi with Bridgestone tyres.

The standard tyres on the early Turbos were Michelins, then Pirellis were used, but now Imprezas are fitted with Bridgestones; the WRX models have come with RE-010, RE-040 and RE-050 tyres, depending on the year of

15in alloy wheels were fitted to the original classic Impreza Turbo 2000.

build (with a 215/45 17 size fitting) while from 2005 onwards, the STi has been fitted with RE-070 tyres (with a 225/45 17 size). There are widely differing opinions within the Impreza community on which are the best alloys and tyres to fit, so be prepared to view models shod with all sort of rubber and gleaming·alloy – just make sure you're happy with their condition.

Wheel condition

Ex Gd Av Po
4 3 2 1

A cursory glance of the wheels will give a good idea of their condition, but look closely to check for kerbing and other scuffs. Small scratches can be sanded out and refurbished, but deeper marks will be more difficult to repair and may be signs of abuse and possible suspension damage. Look through the spokes to check for stone chips and scratches. If you can't see through the alloys clearly, get underneath and have a look – a torch may help. If that's not appealing, you may be able to check further when the car is in the air (see ramp check). This is important, as extensive damage may be the result of some off-road entertainment.

Tyre condition and rating

Ex Gd Av Po
4 3 2 1

Measure the tread depth on each side of the tyres; if there is uneven tyre wear it might just be incorrect tyre pressure, but it may point to bent suspension, wheel misalignments or a damaged bodyshell caused by a crash or abuse. Also look for any nicks or cuts in the tyre walls, as these can signify hard kerbing. The tyre rating will be W or Z; these cover speeds above 150mph. There was some debate previously as to whether or not such a high rating was needed; Subaru used to specify a V rating for speeds up to 150mph, but with the increased performance of the model, particularly the STi, a W or Z rating is the best option.

Hub bearings and steering joints

Ex Gd Av Po
4 3 2 1

Vibration and a grinding noise from the wheels are symptoms of worn hub bearings. They can be examined with the wheel clear of the ground so either use the jack or a ramp check. Pull and push the wheel while turning it and listen for noises and excess movement. Check the constant velocity (CV) gaitor boots on the driveshafts are not split, as this may mean new CV joints are needed. See ramp check for more information.

Interior

Suffice to say that the interiors on the early Impreza turbos were nothing to get excited about. Drab, dreary and grey with plastic that was relatively easy to scratch and mark meant that Subaru was never going to win awards for interior design.

However, things have improved considerably as time has gone on and

Brake dust is common, especially on front wheels, but look beyond this for kerbing marks and scuffs.

Check tyres closely for uneven wear.

Original Impreza interiors were functional but hardly inspiring. A new stereo is this example's lone modification.

Subaru turned the Impreza's cabin into a more pleasurable evironment.

If your search for an Impreza is extensive then expect to see a range of interiors that will differ in look, quality and feel. However, always ensure the interior is in good condition relative to its age and the materials used; in spite of its blandness, a well-sorted interior of a MY95 Turbo could well reflect the owner's overall attitude to his car.

The limited edition WR1 is a superb Impreza – but still very grey inside. (Courtesy Subaru (UK) Ltd)

Seats

Ex Gd Av Po
4 3 2 1

Sports seats have been standard in the Impreza since the facelift classics were introduced. Up until 1996, the grey cloth seats offered little in terms of support whereas the sports seats held the driver more firmly in place – much more fun along twisty country roads.

If the front seats in the earliest models haven't been upgraded by the owner, check for sagging and worn material. The headrests are adjustable and will accommodate most heights. If the seats have been replaced by sportier versions, ensure they have been properly fitted.

Seatbelts are height-adjustable.

STi front seat complete with red stitching.

Post-1996, better cloth on the sports seats improved matters dramatically, while the STis enjoyed blue-black alcantara-syle seats with STi stitched into the seatbacks. These seats are much more supportive, designed to grip the driver firmly in place and therefore withstand the high forces the Impreza can generate when cornering.

The seats move fore and aft, and the handle for this can be found underneath and at the front of the seat. Between the seat and the door is a lever that raises and lowers the seat, and behind that is the lever to adjust the angle of the seat back. CD interchangers can fit underneath the seats.

Seats and interiors have improved considerably, as this STi illustrates. (Courtesy Subaru (UK) Ltd)

The height-adjustable front seatbelts have pretensioners and load limiters with three 3-point belts in the rear. Check the seatbelts fully retract when unbuckled.

If the rear seats fold forwards, they are pulled by release tabs at the top of the seatbacks (they can also be pushed from inside the boot).

Carpet
More grey material, but the quality has improved. The older versions can start to look tatty, but with mats in the front they should not be worn. The carpet can be lifted up, and if there is a CD interchanger or other similar add-ons in the boot, the wiring will run between carpet and floor pan. Check the carpet has been replaced properly.

Headlining/sunroof
There are two sun visors in the front with mirrors which can be moved to shield the door windows. Above each seat is a coat grip/handle. The headlining is generally resilient and should not be sagging, even in the oldest of models. In the middle of the headlining is the interior light with three settings. The WRX SL Imprezas are fitted with sunroofs, as are some of the older Prodrive Style editions.

Door cards/keys/handles

Colour-coded door handles became standard after the classics.

The early Imprezas had black flush handles with a pull-up mechanism. These changed with the launch of the new generation cars when pull-out colour-coded handles were fitted. There is a central locking system that can be operated either by the key or the remote control, which will also set the alarm. Each door can be individually locked from the inside, but the driver's lock will trigger all four. There are also two small locks on each of the rear doors that prevent the doors from being opened from the inside. The two front doors are fitted with speakers. The door cards will be grey material and plastic, although the STi has the blue alcantara fabric to match the seat. If you're presented with a dazzling red-patterned door it is likely to be a Prodrive Style model. Don't worry, your eyes will get used to it.

Door interiors of the classics were easy to scratch and mark.

Electric windows
All the electric windows can be operated and locked by the driver with switches fitted on the door arm rest, although each window can be individually operated. Only the driver's side has a single-switch setting that fully opens the window. The rear windows will open approximately two-thirds of the way down. The windows are frameless, and

at high speed there can be some vibration and whistling, exacerbated by any ageing rubber seals against which the windows press.

Steering wheel

Ex Gd Av Po
[4] [3] [2] [1]

Leather-trimmed Momo steering wheels, complete with airbag, were introduced to the Impreza in 1998. Before that the steering wheels on the classics were large, plastic and unattractive, although to their credit they also had airbags. Subaru has kept the three-spokes with the STi looking slightly more jazzy thanks to the red stitching on the leather. The horn, which is operated from the bottom spoke, is the only extra function on the steering wheel. The height of the steering column is adjustable with the release lever on the left-hand side where the column meets the dash.

Wing mirror and electric window switches on driver's door; check they are functioning properly.

Instrument panel

Ex Gd Av Po
[4] [3] [2] [1]

There have been few changes to the instrument panel in terms of overall look and feel, although an MY07 STi is undoubtedly different to a MY92 WRX. Directly in front of the driver in an early Turbo are two large black dials, one for rpm and the other for mph/kmh. To the left of these is the oil temperature gauge with the fuel gauge on the right. The rear window de-icer button sits next to the fuel gauge, with the electric wing mirror switches and rear fog lamp button beneath. At the same height on the opposite side are the front fog lamp and headlight wiper buttons, with the hazard light button above them. There are two stalk levers on the steering column; the left-hand side operates the windscreen wipers while the headlight settings are on the right-hand lever. Just below this is the slot for the ignition key. Virtually

Impreza WRX instrument panel and Momo steering wheel, with airbags for driver and passenger. (Courtesy Subaru (UK) Ltd)

MY07 STi instrument panel with warning lights on.

underneath the dashboard and close to the driver's door is the bonnet release catch. On top of the steering column is the on-off button for the parking lights. Since the first classics the positioning and colour of the dials has changed and switches have moved, but essentially the format is the same. However, one development needs highlighting; in the STi there is the i/c water spray switch which sprays water onto the intercooler and improves the effectiveness of the turbocharger. Next to the handbrake sits a switch with three height settings for the headlights.

Centre console

Ex Gd Av Po
4 3 2 1

The centre console has three heater controls – for direction, temperature and power. Between them will be buttons for the air-conditioning, if fitted (standard since 2000). Above these are the two main air vents which are supplemented by two at either end of the dashboard, two at feet level and two longer vents across the base of the windscreen. When operational, the air-con works in conjunction with these controls. Below these are the digital clock, the radio-cassette or CD player and cigarette lighter and ashtray. As with the main instrument panel, the location of these features has changed over the years and developed from black plastic to aluminium-effect dials.

DCCD

Ex Gd Av Po
4 3 2 1

Between the front seats of the STi (e.g. STi RA, WR1 and MY2005) sits the manual driver's control centre differential (DCCD). This switch adjusts the amount of torque being generated and at its most extreme can transfer 65% of torque to the rear wheels providing the driver with oversteer. Once the engine is switched off, the system returns to the factory settings.

Gauges

Ex Gd Av Po
4 3 2 1

Apart from the instruments already listed, any other gauges or tachos dotted around the interior will be aftermarket products. These may include oil temperature, exhaust temperature and inlet air temperature gauges, and are usually mounted on the dashboard, in place of the ashtray, or attached to the A-pillar. Whether or not these are useful usually depends on what engine modifications have been made, but owners generally fit them for good reason. A close examination is recommended to ascertain they have been correctly installed, are functioning, and have not damaged the surrounding areas.

Gear shift

Ex Gd Av Po
4 3 2 1

The original five-speed classics had a long shift throw which, although not excessive, did affect the swiftness of gear changes. Housed in rubber casing, the shift just added to the overall cheap feel of the interior. Things improved in 1998 when a shorter throw gearshift with leather trim was introduced and the short-throw lever has remained since. Some owners may have replaced the original gear shift with a shorter stick. These replacements may not necessarily be shorter-throw but rather just shorter sticks and will have to travel just as far as the originals.

When the six-speed STi cars were launched, a pull-up

Inter-cooler water spray button.

STi centre console with gear shift. Note the pull-up mechanism on the shift for engaging reverse.

If you're not already having enough fun in the STi, there's always the manual diff to play with.

reverse mechanism was incorporated into the shift; this consists of a ring beneath the knob that is lifted before the shift is moved into the reverse position.

Pedals

Ex	Gd	Av	Po
4	3	2	1

Pedals were covered by rubber grips on early Turbos but these have since given way to more sporty-looking aluminium pedals. Owners may have had aftermarket pedals fitted, especially on older Imprezas so make sure they have been properly drilled. Check them for wear and tear. There is a footrest to the left of the pedals.

Airbags

Ex	Gd	Av	Po
4	3	2	1

A driver's airbag fitted inside the steering wheel was the only protection in the early models. An airbag for the front passenger was soon included and now dual front side airbags are available as an option. It is important to find out if the car has been involved in a crash, because if so the airbags will have had to be reset. If you end up paying for this 'oversight', it won't come cheap (see chapter 2).

STi aluminium pedals with rubber offer better grip and a sportier look.

Boot (trunk)

Ex	Gd	Av	Po
4	3	2	1

The boot (trunk) release catch is on the floor on the driver's side. This can be disengaged by flicking the 'cancel' switch on the boot-locking mechanism. The boot can then only be opened with the key. There is an internal light which turns on when the boot is opened. CD interchangers are often fitted in the ceiling of the boot cavity, which will impact slightly on storage space.

Spare wheel and toolkit

Ex	Gd	Av	Po
4	3	2	1

The spare wheel and jack handle are located underneath the boot carpet and hard board covering. The tools will also be located here, while the jack is

Rubber protector fitted to Impreza WRX.

Plenty of space in the WRX wagon boot, shown with back seats down. (Courtesy Subaru (UK) Ltd)

Boot carpet lifted back to reveal spare wheel recess in Turbo 2000.

in a pocket behind the lining on the left wall of the boot. The tyre should be a Bridgestone.

Fuel filler

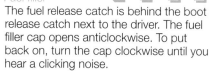

The fuel release catch is behind the boot release catch next to the driver. The fuel filler cap opens anticlockwise. To put back on, turn the cap clockwise until you hear a clicking noise.

Mechanicals
Under the bonnet (hood)

It's a pretty impressive sight underneath the bonnet – it may be baffling but there's no doubt there is a lot going on. The engine bay is dominated by the flat-four boxer engine slung low with the intercooler at the back. There are a number of yellow caps to point to engine parts that the owner can easily inspect; Subaru advises owners not to interfere with other parts unless qualified to do so. The clearly labelled yellow caps are for the brake fluid reservoir, clutch fluid reservoir, power steering fluid reservoir, engine oil filler cap, engine oil level gauge, engine coolant reservoir and windshield washer tank. At the front on the left of the STi is the air intake pipe (not on the classics).

MY94 Turbo 2000 engine showing signs of wear and tear and corrosion. A front strut brace has been added.

Engine mounts

These will wear out after time, causing the engine to vibrate excessively. Problems were reported when Subaru changed the engine mounts in the MY2006 STIs from metal to plastic. Subaru replaced them under warranty with MY2005 metal mounts, and later MY2006 cars were equipped with these as standard. Check closely.

Engine and chassis numbers

The chassis code and 17-digit vehicle identification number (VIN) can be found in the engine bay. The VIN is also marked on the rear firewall of the engine bay. From 2003 onwards, a plastic plate with the chassis number was welded onto the

WRX STi engine with intercooler at back, flat-four layout in red, and air intake pipe at bottom left.

VIN number etched onto driver's side rear
firewall of engine bay.

WRX engine shown with drivetrain and
suspension. (Courtesy Subaru (UK) Ltd)

dash beneath the near-side wiper blade.
The number is visible from the outside.
For more detail, go to chapter 17.

Turbocharger

The turbocharger is oil cooled and must
be cared for. Never switch off the engine
immediately after hard driving, because
the turbocharger needs to cool down
by letting the oil flow through with the
engine idling (also partly achieved by 'normal' driving for a few minutes). If the owner
demonstrates the car to you, just watch how they treat the engine and turbocharger
and then make your mind up. The turbo should be quiet when operating, and there
should be no white smoke from the exhaust when idle.

Exhaust system

Many owners will have had modified exhausts installed, particularly among the
classic drivers who replaced the peashooter twin-pipes with a single tail pipe. They

WRX STi exhaust system shown from
front to back.

Prodrive tail pipe fitted as part of the
Prodrive Performance Pack.

vary in noise but generally make the flat-four engine rumble even louder, so make sure it is something you're happy with. Further exhaust modifications are popular, and these can improve performance considerably, but ensure that there is still a catalytic converter present otherwise the car will fail the MoT. Check the exhaust is not leaking. Another potential 'cat' problem has been reported from MY2002-03 cars in the USA. 'Cats' in the up-pipe were found to deteriorate and fly into the turbo, causing significant turbo damage. A loss of power, slight smoke, shaft play or odd sounds from the turbo are some telltale signs, but the only real way to investigate is to pull off the down-pipe and look at the turbine.

Fuel injection system

Ex 4 Gd 3 Av 2 Po 1

The mass airflow sensor (MAF) is the primary component in the fuel injection system. If the air flow does not hit the sensor correctly, it cannot tell the ECU how much fuel to send to the engine. This was a common problem on 1999/2000 Imprezas and could be detected by a 'flat spot' when driving off from stationary.

ECU

Ex 4 Gd 3 Av 2 Po 1

From 2003, Imprezas were fitted with an adaptive ECU to help with performance and fuel economy. As the car is driven, the ECU remembers how the engine is working and functions accordingly. If more than one person regularly drives the car, however, the ECU can get confused. ECUs are often remapped by owners looking to tune their engines for optimum performance. Remapping on pre-1999 models is not possible because there is not enough memory available. The ECU is located under the passenger footwell. Expert advice is recommended for remapping.

Sparkplugs

Ex 4 Gd 3 Av 2 Po 1

These are difficult to reach, but fortunately can function adequately for around 30,000 miles before they need changing.

Camcover gaskets

Ex 4 Gd 3 Av 2 Po 1

A common problem amongst Imprezas is leaking from the camcover gaskets. If you smell burning oil when driving, it is probably the offside gasket dropping oil onto the exhaust system. This is not a major concern, providing the required oil level is maintained.

Suspension

Ex 4 Gd 3 Av 2 Po 1

The Impreza's suspension consists of MacPherson struts with lower control arms and an anti-roll bar at the front, with trailing arms and another anti-roll bar at the back. Improvements have been made as the car has evolved, with a stiffer chassis helping suspension performance. Inverted damper struts used in the Subaru World Rally Car were incorporated into the STi to further improve the system, resulting in

WRX rear brakes with anti-roll bar link.

superior geometry control and damping performance under hard driving.

The Impreza's suspension is strong, reliable and will generally withstand some serious G-forces. Even so, parts do need replacing, so it is worth checking the anti-roll bar bushes. Cars may have been fitted with aftermarket drop links with harder bushes (probably polyurethane) in order to reduce flexing and increase the rear roll bar stiffness. Look at the bushes first if possible (or check the paperwork to see if they have been replaced). If there is a problem, there may be a clonking noise when driving. Bent or new links and twisted inner front wishbone mounts can point to crash damage or heavy kerbing.

Standard Impreza springs are black but many will have been upgraded using Eibachs, often as part of the Prodrive Performance Pack. WRX upgrades will usually be blue and red for the STi and drop the ride height about an inch. Make sure they have been properly installed.

WRX front brake with suspension springs and MacPherson struts.

To check the condition of the springs or to see if the car has been lowered, measure from the centre of the wheel to the top of the wheelarch. The following table gives the correct distances:

Model year	Saloon (front)	Saloon (rear)	Estate (front)	Estate (rear)
1994-2000	371mm/14.6in	363mm/14.3in	371mm/14.6in	363mm/14.3in
2001-2007	396mm/15.6in	376mm/14.8in	387mm/15.2in	376mm/14.8in

Each measurement has a +/- variable of 12mm

Strut braces

Ex 4 Gd 3 Av 2 Po 1

The STi is fitted with a front strut brace to further stiffen the suspension. Front and rear braces are often fitted to other models by owners with the aim of improving the handling. The rear ones are generally believed to boost the estates (station wagons) because they lack a solid bulkhead. The front braces can be a tight fit, so make sure they are properly installed and have not damaged the bonnet.

Security systems

Ex 4 Gd 3 Av 2 Po 1

Only post-1999 cars were fitted with Category 1 alarms, but with the rising number of thefts insurance companies insisted on them, so Subaru fit them as standard.

Pre-1999 car owners may have had their systems upgraded in order to secure or lower the cost of their insurance. Insurers may also require the car to be equipped with a tracker system. Factor this in to the cost if there isn't one present. The alarm is armed remotely.

Heat shields

Ex	Gd	Av	Po
4	3	2	1

The heat shields are built to withstand an extreme range of temperatures from the Impreza's engines, and pre-1997 cars were known to suffer from cracking problems. However, the problem is not unique to these models and cracks can appear around the mounts. The problem can manifest itself at around 3000rpm when driving.

Steering rack

Ex	Gd	Av	Po
4	3	2	1

The steering system is rack and pinion and generally problem-free. Most models have 2.8 turns lock-to-lock, although the newer STi comes with a quicker steering rack for sharper response and 2.6 turns.

Power steering

Ex	Gd	Av	Po
4	3	2	1

The seals on the power steering reservoir can fail, leading to fluid loss. This has been most common on models from the Bugeyes onwards. The steering will feel stiff and juddery if there is a problem.

Clutch

Ex	Gd	Av	Po
4	3	2	1

The clutch pedal should not be heavy or too high in the movement. Clutch judder from cold is a common occurrence, particularly amongst the classics, but should disappear when the engine is warmed up. Keep the revs low until the engine has reached operating temperature. The clutches can last up to 50,000 miles (80,000km) under normal driving conditions, but their shelf life will drop dramatically with some hard driving or track days.

Gearbox

Ex	Gd	Av	Po
4	3	2	1

The Turbos and WRX are five-speed models, with the six-speed STis launched in 2000. Because of the power the Impreza puts out, the gearboxes take some pressure. Kept as standard, the car should pose few problems for the gearbox, but if the engine has been tuned then the gearboxes can prove fragile under hard driving conditions. Gear changes have improved as the shifts have become short-throw, with the precise STi gears the pick of the bunch. Ensure the gears move freely and there is no slipping.

Differentials

Ex	Gd	Av	Po
4	3	2	1

The Impreza came with an open front differential, viscous coupling centre, and rear differentials with a 50/50 torque split between front and rear.

Gearbox casing in good condition, shown alongside exhaust downpipe.

With the Driver Controlled Centre Differential the driver can dial in the amount of torque required in the rear wheels. The rear differential should be completely oil tight and can be seen without lifting the car by looking underneath from the back. It sits between the steering arms.

Rear diff case should be dry and leak-free as shown here ...

Battery

Ex	Gd	Av	Po
4	3	2	1

The battery is located at the front right of the engine bay. Because it is quite small with plenty of work to perform, it is worth checking the fluid levels and topping up if necessary.

STi engine bay fuse box above battery and windscreen wipers filler cap.

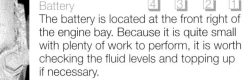

... while this one needs serious attention.

Fuse boxes

Ex	Gd	Av	Po
4	3	2	1

There are two fuse boxes, one under the dashboard (exact location depends on the model year) and the second on the engine bay next to the battery. Look in the owner's manual for individual fuse functions and locations on the boards.

Hoses

Ex	Gd	Av	Po
4	3	2	1

The engine bay is full of hoses attached to the requisite components with metal clips. Check them for leaks, cracks and pliancy; if hard, they may need changing. Replacement hoses are common, with Samco the favoured choice, providing a more colourful engine bay.

Interior fuse board and wiring of MY95 looks untidy compared to ...

... fuse board fitted from 1997. It's hidden behind the compartment housing the alarm keypad, next to the bonnet release catch.

Brakes

The brake discs should be shiny and smooth, although a very light coating of rust may be evident if the car has not been used for some time. However, this should brush off quickly once the wheels are operational. Deeper corrosion is common around the disc rims, particularly if the car is not garaged. Deep pitting of the discs means they will need replacing, as the pads have less surface area to grip with resultant poor braking. If the brake discs have a blue tinge they may be distorted through overheating, which will also impair braking performance.

Brakes are a common modification for owners, especially among owners of the early Turbos fitted with two-pot brakes. Four and six-pot brake upgrades are the most popular, often accompanied by braided hoses. The STi cars were

Brake disc showing clear signs of corrosion.

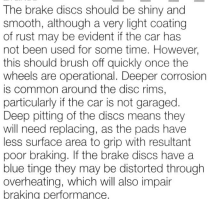

Pockmarked brake disc; if deeper pitting develops, brake performance will deteriorate.

Remember the oil light indicates pressure, NOT level. (Courtesy Subaru (UK) Ltd)

Visually check the brake discs thoroughly for any damage, and test them hard when driving.

fitted with an ABS braking system from Brembo, featuring larger ventilated front and rear brakes with four-pot callipers at the front and twin-pot offset opposed callipers at the rear.

Test drive
Cold start

Ex	Gd	Av	Po
4	3	2	1

Turn the key to start the car, but do not put your foot on the throttle because this can close down the ECU and stop the engine. Don't use high revs (above 3000rpm) until the engine has warmed up. Any blue or white smoke from the exhaust could spell engine or turbo problems respectively.

Warning lights (telltales)

Ex	Gd	Av	Po
4	3	2	1

The warning lights will come on if the ignition key is half-turned but should turn off when the engine is started. The oil warning light is for pressure, not oil level and may not come on until there is very little oil in the system. If the engine warning light is lit the car may go into safe mode, reducing throttle power by 50% to preserve the engine.

Operation clutch

Ex	Gd	Av	Po
4	3	2	1

Clutch judder is fairly common from a cold start. It's caused by the flywheel, drive plate and clutch cover not coming together uniformly. The judder should disappear when the engine is warm. If not, the clutch may need looking at.

Operation gearbox

Ex	Gd	Av	Po
4	3	2	1

The gear positions are well marked on the gear knob on all models. Engaging reverse often requires the clutch to be lifted and lowered again before moving the gear shift. This is not a defect, just the by-product of the gearbox's design. Reverse on the six-speed STi cars requires pulling up the ring around the gear shift before moving it into the reverse position. When driving, gear changes should be smooth, with no whining noises coming from the gearbox.

Steering feel

Ex	Gd	Av	Po
4	3	2	1

The steering should be responsive and precise. If the car moves off the straight line with no steering input, this might signify chassis damage.

Operation brakes

Braking should be powerful and smooth and the car should stop in a straight line. Watch out for juddering when braking as it will be caused by cracked or distorted discs. If there is tugging to either side of the road the brakes may be worn, or worse still, the chassis is damaged. Brake fade is a common occurrence when driving the car hard, while a spongy brake feel can be noticeable on older cars.

Noises

Listen to the engine once the car has been started; it should tick over with its trademark gruff, off-beat throb from the flat-four boxer engine (the off-beat sound is not so marked in the 2.5-litre models though). Any rattling or excessive vibration could mean the engine mounts are weakening. Rattling or buzzing noise from the engine at around 3000rpm may be caused by heatshield cracks. Any clonking noises from underneath can signify worn anti-roll bar bushes or struts. Vibration on the rear view mirror is not uncommon, but it should not be so bad as to impair viewing.

Performance

Resist opening up the throttle above 3000rpm until the engine has reached operating temperature (shown by the temperature gauge resting halfway between hot and cold on the dashboard dial). The engine should be responsive to the throttle for acceleration up the gears, but also within gears. There may be some turbo lag but the response at the top end more than makes up for that, and once you reach 3000rpm and keep going the Impreza rarely fails to impress. In contrast, the car is perfectly capable of sitting in urban traffic.

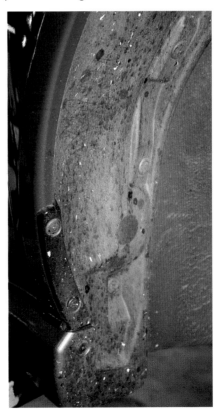

Operation controls and switches

There is some variation of controls among the Impreza models, but overall they follow a similar pattern and are clearly marked. Just try to ensure they are all in working order.

Ramp check

The main things to check underneath when the car is in the air are the wheels. Examine them closely for damage. Minor kerb scuffs are nothing to worry

Examine the wheelarches and wheels for excessive scratches and chips; these are signs of hard off-roading.

about. However, dents, scratches or chips on the spokes or buckled rims might point to a car that has taken some off-road punishment, with gravel and other debris being kicked up by the spinning wheels as they struggle for grip. If mud flaps have been fitted the damage to the wheelarches will be lessened, but look closely to assess their condition with or without the flaps. Any uneven tyre tread wear may be the result of an accident or heavy kerbing, and could mean suspension damage (see Suspension).

Push and pull the wheels while turning them to test the hub bearings; excess movement and a grinding noise could signify that they are worn. Check the CV boots on the driveshafts by turning the wheel and looking for splits or holes in the rubber. If they have perished or split the protective grease will leak out, dirt and grime will get in and new CV joints will be required. Grease on the wheel rims is a possible sign of leakage. Also check for worn anti-roll bar bushes.

Ensure CV gaiter rubber boots are intact.

Bent rear subframe bracket.
(Courtesy Cheam Motors Ltd)

STi fitted with PPP exhaust system.

Examine along the length of the exhaust system; it is well protected but check for any leaks, loose shielding or damage. Also, check there are no leaks from fuel pipes and other components, such as the rear differential.

Check the heat shields for cracks and the front subframe and bottom of the engine for any damage. Make sure the rear subframe brackets are not bent (when driving they can make a knocking sound as the bush hits the bracket).

Look into any cavities for signs of damage or rust.

Evaluation procedure

Add up the total points. Score: **240 = excellent; 180 = good; 120 = average; 60 = poor**. Cars scoring over 170 will be completely useable and will require only maintenance and care to keep in condition. Cars scoring between 60 and 120 will require serious restoration (at much the same cost regardless of score). Cars scoring between 121 and 169 will require very careful assessment of necessary repair/ restoration costs in order to reach a realistic value.

www.velocebooks.com / www.veloce.co.uk
All current books • New book news • Special offers • Gift vouchers

10 Auctions
– sold! Another way to buy your dream

Auction pros & cons
Pros: Prices will usually be lower than those of dealers or private sellers, and you might grab a real bargain on the day. Auctioneers have usually established clear title with the seller. At the venue you can usually examine documentation relating to the vehicle.

Cons: You have to rely on a sketchy catalogue description and history. The opportunity to inspect is limited, and you cannot drive the car. Auction cars are often a little below par and may require some work. It's easy to overbid. There will usually be a buyer's premium to pay in addition to the auction hammer price.

Which auction?
Auctions by established auctioneers are advertised in car magazines and on the auction houses' websites. A catalogue, or a simple printed list of the lots for auctions might only be available a day or two ahead, though often lots are listed and pictured on auctioneer' websites much earlier. Contact the auction company to ask if previous auction selling prices are available as this is useful information (details of past sales are often available on websites).

Catalogue, entry fee and payment details
When you purchase the catalogue of the vehicles in the auction, it often acts as a ticket allowing two people to attend the viewing days and auction. Catalogue details tend to be comparatively brief, but will include information such as 'one owner from new, low mileage, full service history', etc. It will also usually show a guide price to give you some idea of what to expect to pay and will tell you what is charged as a 'buyer's premium'. The catalogue will also contain details of acceptable forms of payment. At the fall of a hammer an immediate deposit is usually required, the balance payable within 24 hours. If the plan is to pay cash there may be a cash limit. Some auctions will accept payment by debit card. Sometimes credit or charge cards are acceptable, but will often incur an extra charge. A bank draft or bank transfer will have to be arranged in advance with your bank as well as with the auction house. No car will be released before all payments are cleared. If delays occur in payment transfers then storage costs can accrue.

Buyer's premium
A buyer's premium will be added to the hammer price: don't forget this in your calculations. It is not unusual for there to be a further state tax or local tax on the purchase price and/or on the buyer's premium.

Viewing
In some circumstances it's possible to view on the day, or days before, as well as in the hours prior to, the auction. There are auction officials available who are willing to help out by opening engine and luggage compartments and to allow you to inspect the interior. While the officials may start the engine for you, a test drive is out of the question. Crawling under and around the car as much as you want is permitted, but

you can't suggest that the car you are interested in be jacked up, or attempt to do the job yourself. You can also ask to see any documentation available.

Bidding

Before you take part in the auction, decide on your maximum bid – and stick to it!

It might take a while for the auctioneer to reach the lot you are interested in, so use that time to observe how other bidders behave. When it's the turn of your car, attract the auctioneer's attention and make an early bid. The auctioneer will then look to you for a reaction every time another bid is made, usually the bids will be in fixed increments until the bidding slows, when smaller increments will often be accepted before the hammer falls. If you want to withdraw from the bidding, make sure the auctioneer understands your intentions – a vigorous shake of the head when he or she looks to you for the next bid should do the trick! Assuming that you are the successful bidder, the auctioneer will note your card or paddle number, and from that moment on you will be responsible for the vehicle.

If the car is unsold, either because it failed to reach the reserve or because there was little interest, it may be possible to negotiate with the owner, via the auctioneers, after the sale is over.

Successful bid

There are two more items to think about. How to get the car home and insurance. If you can't drive the car, your own or a hired trailer is one way, another is to have the vehicle shipped using the facilities of a local company. The auction house will also have details of companies specialising in the transfer of cars.

Insurance for immediate cover can usually be purchased on site, but it may be more cost-effective to make arrangements with your own insurance company in advance, and then call to confirm the full details.

eBay and other online auctions

eBay and other online auctions could land you a car at a bargain price, though you'd be foolhardy to bid without examining the car first, something most vendors encourage. A useful feature of eBay is that the geographical location of the car is shown, so you can narrow your choices to those within a realistic radius of home. Be prepared to outbid in the last few moments of the auction. Remember, your bid is binding and it will be very, very difficult to get restitution in the case of a crooked vendor fleecing you – caveat emptor!

Be aware that some cars offered for sale in online auctions are 'ghost' cars. Don't part any cash without being sure that the vehicle does actually exist and is as described (usually pre-bidding inspection is possible).

Auctioneers

Barrett-Jackson www.barrett-jackson.com, Bonhams www.bonhams.com, British Car Auctions (BCA) www.bca-europe.com or www.british-carauctions.co.uk, Cheffins www.cheffins.co.uk, Christies www.christies.com, Coys www.coys.co.uk, eBay www.ebay.com, H&H www.classic-auctions.co.uk, RM www.rmauctions.com, Shannons www.shannons.com.au, Silver www.silverauctions.com

11 Paperwork
– correct documentation is essential!

The paper trail
Classic, collector and prestige cars usually come with a large portfolio of paperwork accumulated and passed on by a succession of proud owners. This documentation represents the real history of the car, and from it can be deduced the level of care the car has received, how much it's been used, which specialists have worked on it, and the dates of major repairs and restorations. All of this information will be priceless to you as the new owner, so be very wary of cars with little paperwork to support their claimed history.

Registration documents
All countries/states have some form of registration for private vehicles, whether it's like the American 'pink slip' or the British 'log book' systems.

It is essential to check that the registration document is genuine, that it relates to the car in question, and that all the vehicle's details are correctly recorded, including chassis/VIN and engine numbers (if these are shown). If you are buying from the previous owner, his or her name and address will be recorded in the document: this will not be the case if you are buying from a dealer.

In the UK, the current (Euro-aligned) registration document is named "V5C", and is printed in coloured sections of blue, green and pink. The blue section relates to the car specification, the green section has details of the new owner and the pink section is sent to the DVLA in the UK when the car is sold. A small section in yellow deals with selling the car within the motor trade.

In the UK, the DVLA will provide details of earlier keepers of the vehicle upon payment of a small fee, and much can be learned in this way.

If the car has a foreign registration there may be expensive and time-consuming formalities to complete. Do you really want the hassle?

Roadworthiness certificate
Most country/state administrations require that vehicles are regularly tested to prove that they are safe to use on the public highway and do not produce excessive emissions. In the UK, that test (the 'MoT') is carried out at approved testing stations, for a fee. In the USA, the requirement varies, but most states insist on an emissions test every two years as a minimum, while the police are charged with pulling over unsafe-looking vehicles.

In the UK, the test is required on an annual basis once a vehicle becomes three years old. Of particular relevance for older cars, does the certificate issued include the mileage reading at the test date and, therefore, become an independent record of that car's history? Ask the seller if previous certificates are available. Without an MoT the vehicle should be trailored to its new home, unless you insist that a valid MoT is part of the deal. (Not such a bad idea, as at least you will know the car was roadworthy on the day it was tested and you don't need to wait for the old certificate to expire before having the test done.)

Road licence

The administration of every country/state charges some kind of tax for the use of its road system, the actual form of the 'road licence' and, how it is displayed, varying enormously country to country and state to state.

Whatever the form of the 'road licence', it must relate to the vehicle carrying it and must be present and valid if the car is to be driven on the public highway legally. The value of the licence will depend on the length of time it will continue to be valid. In the UK, if a car is untaxed because it has not been used for a period of time, the owner has to inform the licencing authorities, otherwise the vehicle's date-related registration number will be lost and there will be a painful amount of paperwork to get it re-registered. Also in the UK, vehicles built before the end of 1972 are provided with 'tax discs' free of charge, but they must still display a valid disc. Car clubs can often provide formal proof that a particular car qualifies for this valuable concession.

Certificates of authenticity

For many makes of collectible car it is possible to get a certificate proving the age and authenticity (e.g. engine and chassis numbers, paint colour and trim) of a particular vehicle, these are sometimes called 'Heritage Certificates' and if the car comes with one of these it is a definite bonus. If you want to obtain one, the relevant owners club is the best starting point.

If the car has been used in European classic car rallies it may have a FIVA (Federation Internationale des Vehicules Anciens) certificate. The so-called 'FIVA Passport', or 'FIVA Vehicle Identity Card', enables organisers and participants to recognise whether or not a particular vehicle is suitable for individual events. If you want to obtain such a certificate, go to www.fbhvc.co.uk or www.fiva.org; there will be similar organisations in other countries too.

Valuation certificate

Hopefully, the vendor will have a recent valuation certificate, or letter signed by a recognised expert stating how much he, or she, believes the particular car to be worth (such documents, together with photos, are usually needed to get 'agreed value' insurance). Generally such documents should only act as confirmation of your own assessment of the car rather than a guarantee of value as the expert has probably not seen the car in the flesh. The easiest way to find out how to obtain a formal valuation is to contact the owners club.

Service history

Often these cars will have been serviced at home by enthusiastic (and hopefully capable) owners for a good number of years. Nevertheless, try to obtain as much service history and other paperwork pertaining to the car as you can. Naturally, dealer stamps, or specialist garage receipts score most points in the value stakes. However, anything helps in the great authenticity game, items like the original bill of sale, handbook, parts invoices and repair bills all add to the story and the character of the car. Even a brochure correct to the year of the car's manufacture is a useful document and something that you could well have to search hard to locate in future years. If the seller claims that the car has been restored, then expect receipts and other evidence from a specialist restorer.

If the seller claims to have carried out regular servicing, ask what work was completed, when, and seek some evidence of it being carried out. Your assessment of the car's overall condition should tell you whether the seller's claims are genuine.

Restoration photographs

If the seller tells you that the car has been restored, then expect to be shown a series of photographs taken while the restoration was under way. Pictures taken at various stages, and from various angles, should help you gauge the thoroughness of the work. If you buy the car, ask if you can have all the photographs as they form an important part of the vehicle's history. It's surprising how many sellers are happy to part with their cars and accept your cash, but want to hang on to their photographs! In the latter event, you may be able to persuade the vendor to get a set of copies made.

12 What's it worth to you?
– let your head rule your heart!

If the Impreza you've been looking at is particularly poor, it is unlikely that you've used the marking system in chapter 9.

However, if you have got that far you will have a good idea of the car's condition, though still need to make a judgement about the car's value.

There are many motoring magazines and websites with regularly updated price guides, which offer invaluable advice for buyers and sellers. You can also buy price guide booklets which cover more recent models. However, remember that many Imprezas will have modifications that will not be reflected in such listings, except perhaps for those fitted with the official Prodrive Performance Packs.

Modifications can be very desirable and help increase a car's value. Owners who spend thousands on upgrades are unlikely to recoup all their outlay, but can reasonably expect some return. Modifying can become something of an addiction, so it may be cheaper in the long term to buy a car that already has the upgrades. Some modifications are not to everyone's taste, though, and sellers may offer to return the car to standard form, or supply the standard parts they removed.

The Impreza's performance car status has not been reflected in residual values, although later editions are holding up well. Second-hand prices for the earliest or facelift classics are a fraction of their original value, while the limited editions are only marginally better.

New Age or 'Bugeye' Imprezas are worth considering if you're not too concerned with resale value. Their reputation suffered because of appearance, but performance-wise they as worthy of the name Impreza as any other model.

If you are looking for a concours-standard Impreza, hunt out the show owners. So-called 'Show and Shine' is a thriving scene and some examples look as though their wheels have barely turned.

Desirable extras
Prodrive Performance Pack: the official Subaru-approved upgrade. Others are available, but check the supplier's reputation and that the warranty (if appropriate) is still valid.
Alloy wheels: upgraded wheels are near-universal. Gold attracts higher premiums.
Brakes: six-pot brakes or more with braided hoses are common modifications.
Exhaust system: a frequent upgrade, but check the cats are still there.
Interior: leather trim and heated seats in SL models. Elsewhere, seat upgrades and stereo systems are worth looking out for.

Undesirable features
Poorly-fitted and/or cheap-looking body kits, interiors and gauges; engine modifications that don't come with full paperwork.

Doing the deal
So, you know the car's condition, but what about the price? If you think the car is overvalued then haggle – the owner will be expecting it and may respond positively. If you're still unsure of the car's condition, but don't want to let it go, ask for an independent mechanical inspection. If they want to sell, they are unlikely to say no.

Some cars may be best left alone; restoring won't come cheap.

Extensive corrosion has developed on this rear anti-roll bar and its attachment points.

Electricals left to rot may spell further intricate, and, expensive, complications.

Cracked and split hoses in the engine bay could lead to more serious problems.

The first question you need to ask if you are thinking about restoring an Impreza is, 'why bother?'

That is not to say a restoration is not possible, but because there is a healthy supply of good cars available from the earliest Turbos to the GB270, you ought to be able to find one that meets your requirements. Secondly, and perhaps more importantly, if you're thinking of restoring an Impreza's turbo engine then make sure you're either a qualified technician or have access to one, as well having as deep pockets; the Impreza turbo engine is a complicated beast requiring expert attention that will not come cheaply.

Because the Impreza Turbo is a relatively new car (we're only looking back as far as 1992), it is unlikely there will be many examples that have been locked away in deserted barns waiting to be rediscovered and lovingly brought back to life. It's more likely that they will be either on the road and clocking up some hefty mileage by now, or stripped out and in bits in a breakers yard.

Of course, there is the possibility of restoring a modified Impreza to its original virgin condition, but this is still likely to be a lengthy project and may well be a pointless and costly task, considering the availability of unmodified cars on the market. There may be some value in undertaking such a project on a limited edition Impreza, but sourcing original parts may be problematic unless the previous owner held onto them.

If you do want to restore an Impreza then a number of coachbuilding skills will be required on top of the mechanical knowledge already mentioned. Furthermore, you have to ask yourself if you have the appropriate amount of space for your project and the time and patience. These cars were made to be driven and enjoyed; it will be time better spent.

14 Paint problems
– bad complexion, including dimples, pimples and bubbles

Paint faults generally occur due to lack of protection/maintenance, or to poor preparation prior to a respray or touch-up. Some of the following conditions may be present in the car you're looking at.

Orange peel
This appears as an uneven paint surface, similar to the appearance of the skin of an orange. The fault is caused by the failure of atomised paint droplets to flow into each other when they hit the surface. It's sometimes possible to rub out the effect with proprietary paint cutting/rubbing compound or very fine grades of abrasive paper. A respray may be necessary in severe cases. Consult a bodywork repairer/paint shop for advice.

Cracking
Severe cases are likely to have been caused by too heavy an application of paint (or filler beneath the paint). Also, insufficient stirring of the paint before application can lead to the components being improperly mixed, and cracking can result. Incompatibility with the paint already on the panel can have a similar effect. To rectify it is necessary to rub down to a smooth, sound finish before respraying the problem area.

Crazing
Sometimes the paint takes on a crazed rather than a cracked appearance when the problems mentioned under 'cracking' are present. This problem can also be caused by a reaction between the underlying surface and the paint. Paint removal and respraying the problem area is usually the only solution.

Blistering
Almost always caused by corrosion of

This boot lid shows bad prep work from an older paint job – the plastic filler is up to ½in thick in some areas.

Crazing shouldn't affect the original factory paint job.

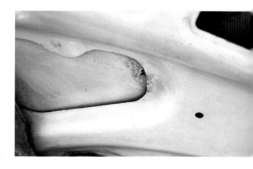

Corrosion underneath the bonnet has resulted in blistering on the surface ...

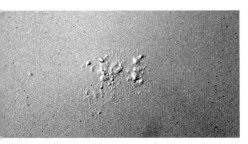

... as shown here.

Colour finish wears off plastic, which then needs repainting.

the metal beneath the paint. Usually perforation will be found in the metal, and the damage will usually be worse than that suggested by the area of blistering. The metal will have to be repaired before repainting.

Micro blistering
Usually the result of an economy respray where inadequate heating has allowed moisture to settle on the vehicle before spraying. Consult a paint specialist, but damaged paint will have to be removed before partial or full respraying. Can also be caused by car covers that don't 'breathe'.

Fading
Some colours, especially reds, are prone to fading if subject to strong sunlight for long periods without the benefit of polish protection. Sometimes, proprietary paint restorers and/or paint cutting/rubbing compounds will retrieve the situation. Often a respray is the only real solution.

Peeling
Often a problem with metallic paintwork when the sealing lacquer becomes damaged and begins to peel off. Poorly applied paint may also peel. The remedy is to strip and start again.

Dimples
Dimples in the paintwork are caused by the residue of polish (particularly silicone types) not being removed properly before respraying. Paint removal and repainting is the only solution.

Dents
Small dents are usually easily cured by the 'Dentmaster', or equivalent process, that sucks or pushes out the dent (as long as the paint surface is still intact). Companies offering dent removal services usually come to your home: consult your telephone directory or the internet.

15 Problems due to lack of use
– just like their owners, Imprezas need exercise!

Fluids
Oil
Withdraw the dipstick and examine the colour and consistency. If golden brown and with no grittiness then all should be OK. If black, the oil is old and will need replacing.

Power steering
All Impreza Turbos have power steering, so check the dipstick in the fluid reservoir (clearly labelled in the handbook and in the engine bay). If very low or empty there may be a leak from the steering rack.

Brakes
With many Imprezas fitted with more powerful brake systems, fluids need to be similarly upgraded (Dot 4 or 5 ratings) and changed regularly, ideally every 12 months (fully synthetic fluids are recommended). If the car has been stood idle for many months or longer, the fluid may be OK, but be prepared to fully flush out the system and replace to be confident.

If deep rust has set in on the brake discs, they will not function properly.

Brakes
If there is a light coating of rust on the discs this should polish off quickly once the car is moving. However, if there is substantial rust with stubborn pockmarked areas, then the corrosion is more severe and the discs may need replacing.

Air-conditioning
Aircons need to be properly maintained. If the system has not been run regularly, even for just a few minutes each month, its effectiveness may be impaired. Give the system a thorough test.

Rotting exhaust systems
The Impreza's exhaust system is robust, but many owners will have opted to install stainless steel downpipes, centre sections and backboxes. These stainless stell items are long-lasting and should pose no rust problems.

16 The Community
– key people, organisations and companies in the Impreza world

As Impreza ownership has grown, the community surrounding it has mushroomed and there are owner's groups in most of Subaru's territories. One of the oldest is the Subaru Impreza Drivers Club (SIDC) in the United Kingdom. Established with a handful of members in 1997, the club is a thriving organisation that offers benefits, merchandise and events for its members. No club is directly affiliated to Subaru, although a number have close ties with the company; in the UK this extends to financial benefits through special deals with the SIDC, as well as discounts with many official and independent Subaru dealers.

One of the biggest attractions of ownership is the huge range of modifications. Considering the power that already exists under the bonnet of a standard WRX, these alterations are not necessarily 'improvements'; rather, they satisfy owners' appetites to squeeze out every last drop of performance they can. And then there is the styling – a virtually limitless market that can prove addictive. Owner's clubs are a rich source of information for modifying.

As well as websites and clubs there are magazines devoted to Subaru, in particular *Subiesport* (USA) and *Total Impreza* (UK).

Motorsport
The Impreza is steeped in motorsport. Making its World Rally Championship debut in 1993, the Impreza rose rapidly to the pinnacle of the sport, winning six world titles. The car's rally pedigree is unquestionable, and it still draws huge support. Away from the rally stages, many clubs provide track day opportunities that allow members to test their cars to their (and the driver's) limits.

Specialists
Subaru has a network of dealers in the relevant countries where customers can expect a high standard of service and expertise, as well as easy availability of parts. A substantial section of the market has been taken over by independent specialists who, as well as dealing with conventional servicing and repairs, also provide the aftermarket modifications that official dealers will not countenance. Official dealers will provide the Prodrive Performance Packs with Subaru's blessing, but for any other modifications head for the independents. For peace of mind, always ensure these outlets employ staff with the appropriate Subaru training; a quick look at enthusiast websites will soon provide recommendations.

Websites
Subaru www.subaru.com
Subaru World Rally Team www.swrt.com
Prodrive www.prodrive.com
Subaru Impreza Drivers Club www.sidc.co.uk
Scoobynet www.scoobynet.com
Subieclub www.subieclub.com
North American Subaru Impreza Owners Club www.nasioc.com
Subaru Impreza GT Club Germany www.impreza-gt-club.de

Subaru Owners Club of South Africa www.subaruclub.co.za
Irish Subaru Drivers Club www.555club.com
Impreza Web Owners Club www.iwoc.co.uk
STi Club Russia www.sti-club.com
Sweden Subaru Impreza Club www.impreza.nu/ssi2
Pleiades (Japan) http://www.lares.dti.ne.jp/~tact/priv/pleiades/
Impreza WRX Club Australia www.wrx.com.au
Subaru Club France www.club-amateurs-subaru.com

Books
Long, Brian – *Subaru Impreza: The Road Car & WRC Story,* Veloce Publishing
Rees, Chris – *You and Your Subaru Impreza,* Haynes Publishing
Robson, Graham – *Rally Giants: Subaru Impreza,* Veloce Publishing
Subaru Impreza Turbo Limited Edition 1994-2000 Extra, Brooklands Books
Subaru Impreza WRC Performance Portfolio 2001-2005, Brooklands Books

Out on the track is a superb way of testing the abilities of you and your Impreza.
(Courtesy John Stewart)

www.velocebooks.com / www.veloce.co.uk
All current books • New book news • Special offers • Gift vouchers

Numbers built

The table gives statistics on a range of Imprezas for Japanese, US, Australian and British markets. Because of the huge range of Impreza variants, the table offers a selection. Prices (see page 5) are those for domestic markets and reflect average exchange rates at the time of writing. There are no official figures from Fuji Heavy Industries for the number of turbo models built. However, 1,260,938 Impreza 2-litre cars had been built up to March 2006, the most up-to-date figures currently available.

Performance

Model	Engine	bhp	Top speed (mph)	0-60 mph	Price
WRX 1992 Japan	1994cc	237	149	4.9sec	10,400
WRX STi 1994 Japan	1994cc	246	145	4.7sec	17,800
Turbo 1994-96 UK	1994cc	208	137	5.8sec	17,499
WRX 1994 Aus	1994cc	208	137	5.8sec	19,100
WRX STi Version II 1994 Japan	1994cc	271	145	4.7sec	18,600
WRX Type RA 1997 Japan	1994cc	276	140	4.8sec	11,400
Turbo 1998-2000 UK	1994cc	215	143	5.6sec	19,765
22B 1998 UK	2212cc	276	149	5.0sec	40,000
WRX 1998 Aus	1994cc	218	137	5.5sec	15,200
P1 1999 UK	1994cc	276	155	4.7sec	31,495
WRX 2000 Japan	1994cc	247	150	5.4sec	15,200
WRX STi 2000 Aus	1994cc	276	137	4.6sec	24,000
WRX 2000 Aus	1994cc	215	140	5.7sec	16,400
WRX 2000-02 UK	1994cc	215	140	5.7sec	21,465
WRX UK 300 2001	1994cc	242	143	5.5sec	24,995
S202 2002 Japan	1994cc	316	150	4.6sec	19,200
WRX 2002 USA	1994cc	227	140	5.7sec	16,700

Model	Engine	bhp	Top speed (mph)	0-60 mph	Price
WRX STi Type UK 2002-05	1994cc	261	152	5.2sec	24,995
WRX STi 2003 USA	2457cc	293	155	4.8sec	19,300
WRX STi Spec C Type RA 2004 Japan	1994cc	320	150	5.1sec	18,500
WRX Club Spec Evo 7 Aus	1994cc	222	140	5.7sec	18,100
WR1 2004 UK	1994cc	320	155	4.3sec	29,995
WRX STi 2005 Aus	1994cc	261	150	5.5sec	23,000
S204 2006 Japan	1994cc	316	150	4.6sec	23,400
WRX TR 2006 USA	2457cc	227	140	5.8sec	13,000
WRX 2006-07 UK	2457cc	226	143	5.4sec	20,900
WRX STi 2006-07 UK	2457cc	276	158	5.0sec	26,995
WRX 2007 USA	2457cc	227	140	5.8sec	12,500
WRX 2007 STI USA	2457cc	293	155	4.8sec	16,700
RB270 2007 UK	2457cc	266	143	5.2sec	22,995

The following specifications (unless otherwise stated) are for the base editions of the saloon classic Turbo 2000 and the new generation WRX. The two sets of specifications represent the beginning and end of the Impreza (before the introduction of the new body shape in 2008).

Engine
Impreza Turbo 2000 (1994)
Type: 1994cc horizontally opposed four-cylinder, mounted longitudinally, front, aluminium head and block, turbocharger with air-cooled intercooler
Bore/stroke: 92/75mm
Compression ratio: 8.0:1
Valves: four per cylinder, double overhead camshafts on each bank
Ignition: electronic
Induction: multi-point fuel injection
Power output: 208bhp (211ps)@6000rpm
Torque: 201lb-ft (270Nm)@4800rpm

Impreza WRX (2007)
Type: 2457cc horizontally opposed four-cylinder, mounted fore and aft, aluminium alloy cylinder block and heads, 4 valves per cylinder, double overhead camshafts per bank, turbocharger with air-cooled intercooler, active valve

control system (AVCS)
Bore/stroke(mm): 99.5x79.0
Compression ratio: 8.4:1
Fuel system: multi-point fuel injection, computer-controlled management system
Power: 226.6bhp (230ps)@5600rpm
Torque: 236lb-ft (320Nm)@3600rpm

Transmission
Impreza Turbo (1994)
Permanent four-wheel drive, front differential, centre viscous coupling
Gearbox: five-gear manual
Gear ratios mph per 1000rpm: 1st 3.45/4.8 2nd 1.95/8.6 3rd 1.37/12.2 4th
    0.97/17.2 5th 0.74/22.5 final drive 4.11

Impreza WRX (2007)
Permanent four-wheel drive, centre differential with viscous coupling; dry single plate
    diaphragm clutch; limited slip rear differential with viscous coupling
Gearbox: five-gear manual synchromesh
Gear ratios mph per 1000rpm: 1st 3.45/5.0 2nd 1.95/8.9 3rd 1.37/12.7 4th
    0.97/17.8 5th 0.74/23.5 final drive 4.11

Suspension and steering
Impreza Turbo (1994)
Suspension (front): MacPherson struts, coil springs, transverse link, anti-roll bar
Suspension (rear): MacPherson struts, coil springs, transverse link, trailing arms,
    anti-roll bar
Steering: rack-and-pinion, power-assisted, lock-to-lock 2.8 turns
Turning circle: 10.4m

Impreza WRX (2007)
Suspension (front): MacPherson struts, coil springs, L-shaped transverse link strut,
    anti-roll bar, forged aluminium lower arms
Suspension (rear): MacPherson struts, dual link, coil springs, trailing arms, anti-roll
    bar
Steering: rack-and-pinion, speed sensitive variable-capacity power assistance with
    anti kick-brake damper valve, lock-to-lock 2.75 turns
Turning circle 11.0m

Brakes
Impreza Turbo (1994)
ABS system
Front: ventilated discs with twin-pot callipers
Rear: 230mm solid discs with sliding pot calliper

Impreza WRX (2007)
4-sensor, 4-channel ABS with electronic brakeforce distribution
Ventilated four-pot front and two-pot rear
Dual circuit diagonally split hydraulic system with pressure limiting valve and vacuum servo

Dimensions
The major dimensions increased as the Impreza developed but not to a significant degree.
Impreza Turbo (1994)
Length: 4340mm/171in
Width: 1690mm/66.5in
Height: 1400mm/55in
Weight: 1235kg/2723lb
Wheelbase: 2520mm/99.25in
Luggage capacity: 353 litres/93.25 gallons
Front track: 1460mm/57.5in
Rear track: 1455mm/57.25in
Wheels: 6x15in alloy

Impreza WRX (2007)
Length: 4465mm/175.75in
Width: 1740mm/68.5in
Height: 1440mm/56.75in
Wheelbase: 2525mm/99.5in
Weight: 1405kg/
Luggage capacity: 401 litres/106 gallons
Front track: 1485mm/58.5in
Rear track: 1480mm/58.25in
Wheels: 7x17in alloy

Electrical
Impreza Turbo (1994) and WRX (2007)
Battery: 12V 48Ah
Alternator: 12V 75A

Chassis numbers
The model code and 17-digit vehicle identification number (VIN) can be found in the engine bay. The VIN is also marked on the rear firewall of the engine bay. From 2003 onwards, a plastic plate with the chassis number was welded onto the dash beneath the near-side wiper blade. The number is visible from the outside. Check that the code on the plate matches up with the code in the registration documents.

Model codes consisted of seven characters, as follows:
Model code – 'G' for Impreza
Body type – 'C' for saloon, 'F' for estate (station wagon)
Engine type – '8' for 2.0-litre turbo
Year code – 'B' for Model Year 1994, 'C' for MY95/96, 'D' for MY97, 'E' for MY98, 'F' for MY99, 'G' for MY2000
Door option – '2' for two-door, '4' for four-door saloon (sedan), '5' for five-door estate (station wagon)
Model type – '8' for WRX, '7' for RA, 'E' for STi (version III onwards), 'D' for STi Type R and RA, 'S' for 22B
Transmission – 'D' for five-speed manual, 'P' for four-speed auto

The **Essential** Buyer's Guide™

978-1-904788-69-0

978-1-904788-98-0

978-1-84584-135-5

978-1-84584-136-2

978-1-845840-99-0

978-1-845841-07-2

978-1-845840-29-7

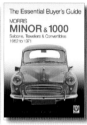
978-1-845841-01-0

978-1-904788-70-6

978-1-84584-146-1

978-1845840-77-8

978-1-904788-85-0

978-1-84584-138-6

978-1-845841-19-5

978-1-845841-13-3

978-1-84584-147-8

978-1-84584-134-8

978-1-845840-26-6

978-1-904788-72-0

978-1-845840-22-8

£9.99*/$19.95*

Also from Veloce ...

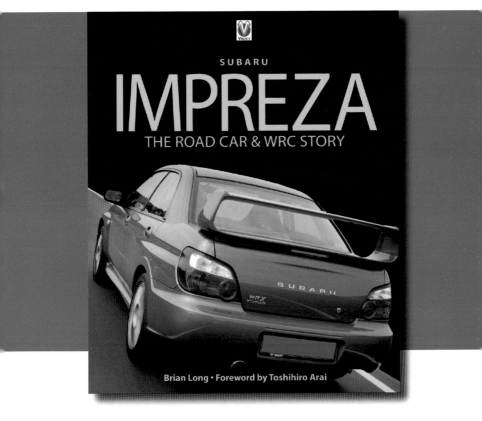

£29.99* hardback • ISBN 978-1-845840-28-0
£19.99* paperback • ISBN 978-1-845840-33-4

Here is the history of the Subaru Impreza, including its fascinating early heritage; the background to the car; the full story of the myriad models in Japan and major export markets, and round-by-round coverage of the Impreza's WRC challenge.
Perceived as a replacement for the long-running Leone, the Impreza quickly gained a good reputation through Subaru's successful WRC programme. This book covers the full story, from concept through to the current production car, looking at the rally machines along the way, and illustrated throughout with contemporary material. Subaru's co-operation with the author has ensured an unrivalled level of detail and accuracy.

This book is available in both hardback (plus dust jacket) and paperback editions. The content of both versions is identical.

Subaru

Impreza

Graham Robson

£14.99*
ISBN 978-1-845840-42-6
This book describes the birth, development, and rallying career of the Subaru Impreza, providing a compact and authoritative history of where, when and how it became so important to the sport.

Audi

Quattro
Group B
Sport
Sport S1

Graham Robson

£14.99*
ISBN 978-1-84584-141-6
This book describes the birth, development, and rallying career of the Audi Quattro, which brought new standards to the sport in the early eighties, providing a compact and authoritative history of where, when and how it became so important to rallying.

*prices subject to change • p&p extra • for more details visit www.veloce.co.uk or email info@veloce.co.uk

Index

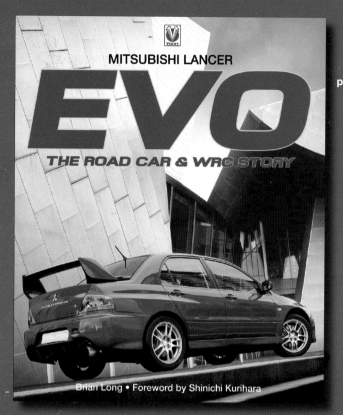

MITSUBISHI LANCER
EVO
THE ROAD CAR & WRC STORY

Brian Long • Foreword by Shinichi Kurihara

£29.99* hardback • ISBN 978-1-84584-055-6
£19.99* paperback • ISBN 978-1-84584-063-1

The Lancer name conjures up many images. For some, it evokes the first generation cars which fought with the best on the Safari Rally and came out the victors. Others will remember the second generation models, and who could not be aware of the Evolution (Evo) series, launched in 1992? The Lancer Evolution is not only one of the greatest rally cars of all time, it is also a desirable high-performance road car. Written in Japan with the full cooperation of Mitsubishi, this is the definitive story of all the world's Lancers, whether they carried Mitsubishi, Dodge, Colt, Plymouth, Valiant, Eagle, Proton or Hyundai badges.